We
Inherited
Lies

A Chiastic Structure Study
of The Revelation of Jesus Christ

Russell McCann & Shirley McCann

LUCIDBOOKS

We Inherited Lies: A Chiastic Structure Study of The Revelation of Jesus Christ

Copyright © 2025 by Russell McCann and Shirley McCann

Published by Lucid Books in Houston, TX
www.LucidBooks.com

Unless otherwise indicated, scripture quotations are taken from the King James Version (KJV): King James Version, public domain.

ISBN: 978-1-63296-872-2
eISBN: 978-1-63296-873-9

Special Sales: Most Lucid Books titles are available in special quantity discounts. Custom imprinting or excerpting can also be done to fit special needs. Contact Lucid Books at Info@LucidBooks.com

Contents

Introduction

Our Why

Tell us, when shall these things be? and what shall be the sign of thy coming, and of the end of the world? And Jesus answered and said unto them, Take heed that no man deceive you.

—Matthew 24:3–4

The disciples asked Jesus these questions, and mankind continues to ask: What are the signs of Jesus Christ's return and of the end of the world? Will the end of the world be with nuclear war, climate change, or an asteroid? Can man control the events that might bring the end of the world?

The book of Revelation is probably the most misunderstood and most debated book of the entire Bible. Everyone believes their interpretation is correct, but these ideas have led to much confusion and deception. Many have been led to believe that the book of Revelation cannot be understood;

therefore, they think it should not be read. Jesus tells John the exact opposite: *"Blessed is he that readeth, and they that hear the words of this prophecy, and keep those things which are written therein: for the time is at hand"* (Revelation 1:3).

Jesus wants all to know that blessed or happy is the man who reads or hears the words of the Revelation. Jesus encourages believers to read and keep or ponder the message of the book, which will give great comfort in troubled times before His return.

We Inherited Lies: A Chiastic Study of the Revelation of Jesus Christ is to be used as a companion text as you read the book of Revelation. No book or person can replace the Word of God. Our goal is to remove any intimidation you may feel when reading the book of Revelation. It is not our intent to give definitive interpretations for every verse; instead, our goal is to present a broader understanding of the book. We address big questions, such as: Who is the antichrist? What is a beast? What is the mark of the beast? How much time do we have left? Our intent is to use Scripture and history to highlight the events spoken of in the Revelation.

The most important goal we hope to accomplish is to make the Revelation of Christ easier to understand. The book of Revelation was originally written as a chiasmus. Therefore, this commentary will emphasize the book's chiastic structure instead of commenting on each verse or chapter. We chose to cite Scripture only from the King James Version because the translators of the King James Version in 1611 were careful to maintain the true meaning of the original text. Instead, of commenting on each verse, we focus on those passages that highlight the Chiasmus.

Our vision is to give you a jumping off point to study the book for yourself and to understand that the Bible is a book that explains itself. Jesus told his disciples to search the Scriptures (John 5:39). Paul admonished Timothy to study the Scriptures for understanding of the doctrines and to increase his faith in God (2 Timothy 2:15; 3:16–17). We will quote the chiasmus Scriptures and reference many more pertinent Scriptures. We urge you to read all reference Scriptures for context to get a better understanding of the message. We also encourage you to google every historical name or event cited for further research.

Our Method

Chiastic Structure in the Book of Revelation

The chiastic structure is easy to understand, but it does change the way we usually read Scripture. The dictionary definition of *chiasmus* refers to a sequence of words in a sentence or verse that are then repeated and developed but in reverse order. Because of its chiastic structure, the book of Revelation is not meant to be read from beginning to end, Chapters 1 to 22. The prophet Isaiah taught that the Bible is to be studied precept upon precept, line upon line:

> Whom shall he teach knowledge? and whom shall he make to understand doctrine? them that are weaned

from the milk. . . . For precept must be upon precept, precept upon precept; line upon line, line upon
line; here a little, and there a little.

—Isaiah 28:9–10

Revelation is not a study for those who continue to need
"milk" or the very elementary teachings of the Word of
God. This study is for the serious Bible student who desires
to dig deeper into God's truth. The phrase *precept upon precept* refers to the doctrines that regulate one's thoughts and
behaviors. The phrase *line upon line* refers to the patterns
of words that biblical writers use to record God's truth. A
deeper understanding of the Word is gained by prayerfully
searching God's Word; every reading increases one's knowledge—"here a little, and there a little."

For our study of the Revelation, we quote a sequence of
words from a verse that are repeated and developed in a later
verse or chapter but in reverse order. This pattern is easier to
identify than it sounds, and the chiasmus adds clarity to the
Scriptures. As you approach the book of Revelation, think
about a triangle. The base line of the triangle is Jesus Christ
who is the beginning and the end, the foundation of the
Bible. On the left arm of the triangle are the history chapters,
1–11, which detail man's history on earth from the time of
John, the apostle and revelator, until the Second Coming of
Christ. On the right arm of the triangle are the eschatologi-
cal chapters, 13–22; these chapters detail the final events of
humanity's time on earth and God's judgment on believers

and unbelievers. Overall, Chapters 1–11 deal with what is happening on earth; Chapters 13–22 look at heavenly scenes that affect what happens on earth and into eternity in the new heaven and earth.

The repetition of ideas and scenes from the left arm to the right arm complements, contrasts, or mirrors the previously stated verse or chapter. For example, the first chapter of Revelation is a chiasmus to the last chapter; both chapters describe Jesus Christ. We title these chapters: "Revelation 1: The First and the Last" and "Revelation 22: The Beginning and the End."

Revelation 12 is the chiasmus climax, and the climax verse is Revelation 12:7, "And there was war in heaven." This is the first event that brought about the conflict between Jesus Christ and Satan. The war began in heaven and continues on earth until the end of man's time on earth. Thus, we begin our study with the climax, Revelation 12:7: "And there was war in heaven."

The chiastic verses are identified as First Chiasmus, Second Chiasmus, and so on. Key words in the verses are highlighted for emphasis. The highlighted words of the chiasmus in the first chapter are in bold font. The words in the repeated chapter are in bold and italic font. For example, the chiasmus in Revelation chapter 1 and chapter 22 would look like this.

First Chiasmus

- **Revelation 1:3**: "**Blessed is he that readeth,** and they **that hear the words** of this prophecy."

- **Revelation 22:7**: "*Blessed is he that keepeth the sayings* of the prophecy of this book."

Suggestions for Getting the Most Benefit from this Study

- Read each Chiasmus as one section.

- Read the bold, italic, and underlined portions of Scripture as one complete thought.

- Take note the highlighted words identify the chiasmus.

- Our commentary expounds on each chiasmus.

- Read reference Scriptures to enhance your understanding.

The Bible Explains the Bible

The Word of God is God's Word. The Word of God is truth and is a witness of itself. We reference and quote many Scriptures to establish the truth of God. Matthew 18:16 says, "But if he will not hear thee, then take with thee one or two more, that in the mouth of two or three witnesses every word may be established." Here are examples of the Word being a witness of itself:

- **Zechariah 12:10**: "And **they shall look upon me whom they have pierced**."

- **John 19:34: "But one of the soldiers with a spear pierced his side."**

John identifies Jesus Christ as the one pierced from Zechariah's prophecy although neither verse uses the name of Jesus Christ. John is describing the crucifixion of Christ as he is observing the event. Zechariah is foretelling the event. Both verses establish that Jesus Christ was pierced in his side.

Our Aim

Our aim is to proclaim the message of hope that this blessed book offers as it comforts God's people in times of trouble like ours. We need this book more than ever as man's history unfolds. Our aim is that all who read this book will find peace in our Lord Jesus Christ as we have through careful study of this book.

After Jesus Christ completed His work of redemption, he rose from the dead, and returned to heaven to sit at the Father's right hand. The book of Revelation covers man's journey on earth from the resurrection of Christ to His Second Coming. In this revelation, Jesus gave John a complete vision of that time; it is a journey filled with love, protection, and guidance from God to his disciples. But it is a journey of confusion, trouble, and fear for those who reject God. God always tells the truth and leaves the choice to man. With this book, it is our heartfelt desire to present this journey clearly and truthfully using the Word of God and history as our references. We do not want to add or take away from the Scriptures; we seek only to enhance the reader's understanding of the Word of God. We prayerfully submit our efforts for the glory of our Heavenly Father.

Biblical Prophetic Terms

The writers of Scripture used imagery and figurative language to help the reader visualize ideas that may be confusing to modern readers. Many of these images are identified in Scripture and remain a constant means of identification throughout the Bible. The following prophetic terms are used in this study. The words in bold italics in the quoted Scripture identify or define the term. We believe that God's words explain God's Word.

Beast: An earthly kingdom.

> **Daniel 7:17**: "These great ***beasts***, which are four, ***are four kings***, which shall arise out of the earth."

Horn: Kingdom, King.

> **Daniel 8:21**: "The ***great horn*** that is between his eyes ***is the first king***."

Mark: Sign, identifier.

> **Exodus 31:13**: "For *it is a sign between me and you* throughout your generations; *that ye may know that I am the Lord that doth sanctify you.* "

> **Romans 4:11**: "And he received the *sign* of circumcision, a *seal of the righteousness* of the faith."

Mountain: A kingdom.

> **Daniel 2:35**: "And the *stone that smote the image became a great mountain*, and filled the whole earth."

Name: Character

> **Exodus 34:6**: "And the Lord passed by before him, and proclaimed, *The Lord, The Lord God, merciful and gracious, longsuffering, and abundant in goodness and truth.*"

Prostitute; Prostitution: Idolatry

> **Leviticus 17:7**: "And they shall *no more offer their sacrifices unto devils*, after whom they have *gone a whoring.*"

> **Judges 2:17**: "And yet they would not hearken unto their judges, but they went a *whoring after other gods and bowed themselves unto them.*"

> **James 4:4**: "Ye *adulterers and adulteresses*, know ye not that the friendship of the world is enmity with God?"

Rock: Jesus Christ

> **Deuteronomy 32:4**: "*He is the Rock*; his work is perfect."

> **1 Corinthians 10:4**: "For they drank of that spiritual Rock that followed them: and *that Rock was Christ.*"

Trees: Individuals

> **Mark 8:24**: "And he looked up, and said, *I see men as trees*, walking."

Trumpet: War

> **Jeremiah 4:19**: "*The* **sound of the trumpet, the alarm of war.**"

Water, sea: Nations; people

> **Revelation 17:15**: "And he saith unto me, The *waters* which thou sawest, where the whore sitteth, *are peoples, and multitudes, and nations, and tongues.*"

White linen: Righteousness

> **Revelation 19:8**: "Clean and *white*: for the *fine linen is the righteousness of saints.*

Wind: War

> **Jeremiah 49:36–37**: "I bring *the four winds* from the four quarters of heaven, ... *I will send the sword after them*, till I have consumed them."

Woman: Church

> **Jeremiah 6:2**: "I have likened the *daughter of Zion to a comely and delicate woman.*"

> **John 3:29**: "He that hath *the bride* is the *bridegroom.*"

> **Ephesians 5:23**: "*Christ is the head of the church.*"

Zion: God's people

> **Isaiah 51:16**: "*Zion, Thou art my people.*"

In prophetic Scripture, one day equals one prophetic year.

> **Genesis 29:27**: "**Fulfil her week**, and we will give thee this also for the service which thou shalt serve with me yet **seven other years**."

> **Numbers 14:34**: "After the number of days in which ye searched the land, even *forty days, each day for a year*, shall ye bear your iniquities, even *forty years*, and ye shall know my breach of promise."

> **Ezekiel 4:6**: "And when thou hast accomplished them, lie again on thy right side, and thou shalt bear the iniquity of the house of Judah *forty days*: I have appointed thee *each day for a year.*"

War in Heaven

What Does This Mean?

War in heaven!! How could there be war in heaven? We envision heaven as the perfect place filled with the presence and the goodness of God. War?? Who fought? Why?

The war in heaven was fought between Jesus Christ and His angels and Satan and his angels. Why was Satan allowed to wage war against Christ? How did Satan get angels?

God, the Creator of all things, loves His creation and deserves worship from all his creation. The war in heaven was not a war fought with weapons, but a war of wills. God created His angels with freedom of choice to worship the Creator. The created being, Lucifer, full of pride rebelled. Lucifer coveted worship, so he refused to worship Christ. Lucifer enticed a third of the angels to join him in his rebellion. What was the outcome of his rebellion?

Jesus Christ prevailed and cast Satan and his demons

from heaven. The war that began in heaven came to earth. Why was it not contained in heaven?

God created angels with free will. God is love, and love does not demand or force faithfulness. Love produces faithfulness which, in turn, produces obedience. The direct response to love, faithfulness, and obedience is worship. The angels had freedom of choice to love and obey God. One-third of the angels chose to believe Lucifer's lies, and Lucifer along with his disobedient angels were cast from the presence of God. Satan brought his war over worship to earth. How did the war affect God's creation on earth?

God created man and woman with free will. Satan began his battle of worship with Eve. Satan, disguised as the serpent in the Garden of Eden, introduced doubt of God's word to Eve's pure and innocent mind. "Yea, hath God said" (Genesis 3:1) are his first words to Eve. Satan's question caused Eve and Adam to doubt God's word, which led to a lack of faith in God and disobedience to their Creator. Adam and Eve made the choice to believe the words of the serpent instead of the words of God. They willingly and freely chose to doubt God's love and provision for them, lost their faith in God, and disobeyed God's commandment. Disobedience of God's Word is sin.

Since the Garden of Eden, man has continued to struggle with sin. Sin brings death. Faith and obedience to God bring eternal life. Jesus Christ, God in the flesh, came to earth to pay the penalty for man's disobedience to God. Man overcomes sin through faith in the saving blood of Jesus Christ by confessing that Jesus Christ is Lord. Who do you choose to believe? Your belief determines who you will worship.

Revelation 12:7 and 12:11 present a contrast between war and victory.

First Chiasmus

- **Revelation 12:7**: "And there was **war in heaven**: Michael and his angels fought against the dragon; and the dragon fought and his angels."

- **Revelation 12:11**: "And *they overcame him by the blood of the Lamb, and by the word of their testimony*; and they loved not their lives unto the death."

"There was war in heaven" begins our study of the book of Revelation. The war in heaven was fought between Michael and his angels against the dragon and his angels. The dragon is also known as Satan, the devil, and Lucifer. Michael is Jesus Christ.

Daniel 10:21: "Michael your prince."

Daniel 12:1: "And at that time shall Michael stand up, the great prince which standeth for the children of thy people: and there shall be a time of trouble, such as never was since there was a nation even to that same time: and at that time thy people shall be delivered, every one that shall be found written in the book."

Matthew 24:21: "For then shall be great tribulation, such as was not since the beginning of the world to this time, no, nor ever shall be."

I Thessalonians 4:16: "For the Lord himself shall descend from heaven with a shout, with the voice of the archangel, and with the trump of God."

The angelic beings and humans are created by God. God is no respecter of persons (Romans 2:11). God does not place any angel or person higher than another. All are equal and the same in Christ. God is the Supreme Authority over His creation. Michael is the prince of the people of God. God alone is the King; Christ is His Prince. No created being whether a man or an angel is given this title. God does not give His glory to another. Michael is one of the names describing the attributes of Christ. Michael means "who is like God" or "gift from God." Paul declares that Christ "thought it not robbery to be equal with God" (Philippians 2:6). Michael, who like God as the Creator of all things, is the only one who can stand for any people.

When Michael stands, there shall be a time of trouble or great tribulation that has never happened or will ever happen again. At that time, Christ will descend from heaven with a shout, with the voice of the archangel, and with the trump of God leading the armies of Heaven. These three sounds describe the event of the Second Coming of Christ. The shout from God is the same as the voice of the archangel; therefore, Michael must be God. The people of God whose names are written in the Lamb's book of life will be delivered. The Son of Man, Jesus Christ, shall send forth his angels to gather the elect from all over the earth (Matthew 24:31). Michael is Jesus Christ.

The war in heaven began when Lucifer declared in his heart:

> **I will** ascend into heaven, **I will** exalt my throne above the stars of God: **I will** sit also upon the mount of the congregation, in the side of the north: [14] **I will** ascend above the heights of the clouds, **I will** be like the most High.
>
> —Isaiah 14:13–14

Why would Lucifer think he could sit on God's throne replacing Jesus Christ? God created man perfect without a sin nature. Paul states in the book of Hebrews that Jesus Christ was "made a little lower than the angels" (Hebrews 2:9). Jesus Christ as Immanuel, God in the flesh, humbled himself to become a mortal man. The Creator of man assumed the role of a man to identify with His creation. He became lower than the angels so He could taste death for man. Christ did this because God so loved His creation that He did not want it to perish from the effects of sin. The omniscient God knew that man would sin; therefore, God's plan for redemption was in place before the world was created (Revelation 13:8).

God created Lucifer as a beautiful covering cherub set by the throne of God. Lucifer was perfect in all his ways until iniquity was found in his heart (Ezekiel 28:14–15). In Revelation, John sees Jesus Christ as the bloody, slain lamb in heaven (Revelation 5:6). Lucifer saw the Lamb slain before the creation of man (Revelation 13:8); in his evil heart, he may have been repulsed by the ugliness of the slain lamb. Lambs are meek and gentle; Lucifer may have seen himself as stronger than the Lamb. In his devious mind, he may have thought that he deserved the most prominent place in heaven and not the ugly, weak Lamb.

"Thou shall not covet" is the gateway sin (Exodus 20:17). God knew that Lucifer coveted the seat of Christ in heaven and the seat of Christ in the church, "the mount of the congregation" (Isaiah 14:13). Satan's intense desire for what he did not deserve led to his wicked action of defying God. He convinced himself and a third of the angels that he could overthrow the slain Lamb of God. Jesus told the Pharisees that "he [Lucifer] was a murderer from the beginning" and that he was the father of lies (John 8:44). Satan's desperately wicked heart made him the classic "rebel without a cause."

While teaching His sermon on the mount, Jesus quoted this commandment: "Thou shalt not kill" (Exodus 20:13). Very few people commit murder, but "whosoever is angry with his brother without a cause shall be in danger of judgment" (Matthew 5:22). Jesus wanted the multitudes to understand that man is in a spiritual battle against good and evil. The battle begins in the heart; what we desire determines what we believe, and what we believe determines our actions. Lucifer had no cause to be angry with Jesus Christ, but his anger raged hot. Lucifer desired the seat of Christ; his heart was lifted up because of his great beauty (Ezekiel 28:11–19). His pride corrupted his wisdom and filled his wicked heart with contempt. Pride filled him with vain words and violence against the Son of God. Lucifer falsely believed that he deserved the seat next to God and the worship given to Christ. The hate in his heart drove him to lie and deceive the angels who followed him from heaven. Satan now desires to draw all men away from the kingdom of God.

Why wasn't Lucifer destroyed when he began his rebellion? Lucifer, along with all the angels and mankind, was created with free will. God's character is love, and He loves all his creation and does not want any to perish. God's character produces love, faithfulness, and obedience. A tyrant produces hate, fear, and rebellion. If God had immediately eliminated Lucifer at the start of his rebellion, all God's creation would have seen a tyrant, not a loving Creator. Lucifer would have been a martyr in heaven, and all the false accusations that he was making about Christ would have appeared to be true.

Lucifer, created perfectly, was in the perfect, loving presence of God, and because of his beauty (Ezekiel 28:17), he chose to lift himself above the Son of God. Lucifer's heart was filled with hate for Jesus Christ; he was accusing Christ of the same malice that was in his own heart. God's heart was broken that his "anointed cherub" (Ezekiel 28:14) would rebel. However, God had no choice but to cast the evil Lucifer and all the angels who followed him from heaven.

How did the war in heaven end? Revelation 12:11 says, "And they overcame him by the blood of the Lamb, and by the word of their testimony."

Jesus Christ also came to earth to live a perfect life before man showing God's love and mercy to all. Jesus Christ willingly, as God's "only begotten Son," gave his life as a ransom for many for the payment of sin. The wages of sin is death, and Jesus willingly with great love for man paid that price for all (Romans 6:23). Anyone who accepts the free gift of eternal life from Christ wins the war of good and evil. Christ prevails. His blood sacrifice is the power of God unto salvation (Romans 1:16). The angelic host who remained in heaven stood firm in their testimony that Jesus Christ is the Son of God. The testimony of Christ is the power of God for the forgiveness of sin. Sinful man cleansed by the blood of the Lamb can stand before God justified, clothed in His righteousness. Eternal life is God's gift to man, and it is God's will that none perish, but that all accept His gift through the sacrifice of Jesus Christ. The entire Word of God testifies of the redeeming work of Jesus Christ.

The war ended on the cross of Calvary. Only the blood of Christ secured the victory over Satan. When Jesus cried, "It is finished," the war in heaven was won.

Second Chiasmus

- **Revelation 12:8**: "And **prevailed not; neither was their place found any more in heaven.**"

- **Revelation 12:9**: "And **the great dragon was cast out**, that old serpent, called the Devil, and Satan, which deceiveth the whole world: **he was cast out into the earth, and his angels were cast out with him.**"

- **Revelation 12:10**: "*Now is come salvation, and strength, and the kingdom of our God, and the power of his Christ: for the accuser of our brethren is cast down*, which accused them before our God, day and night."

Jesus Christ won the war in heaven on the cross. Satan fulfilled his desire to murder Christ at the cross. Satan and his angels were forever cast out of heaven from the presence of God to earth. All God's perfect creation is cursed by the effects of sin because of Satan's desire to replace the Messiah. The justice of God for His creation calls for a remedy for sin. Christ willingly accepted the will of God to redeem all that was lost. Jesus Christ shed his blood on the cross of Calvary so that God's creation could be restored to its former glory. The angels who remained in heaven are vindicated in their decision to worship Christ by the blood of the Lamb. Fallen, sin-cursed humanity is offered redemption by faith in the blood of Jesus Christ. John 12:31–32: "Now is the judgment of this world: now shall the prince of this world be cast out."

Christ defeated Satan on the cross of Calvary. After Jesus Christ's death, burial, and resurrection, He entered heaven with His shed blood and sprinkled it on the altar in heaven completing the work of redemption (Hebrews 9:12). Salvation has come to God's creation through the power of Christ. Jesus Christ has paid the wages of sin for all of mankind. Any individual who believes that Jesus paid the price of sin "should not perish, but have everlasting life" (John 3:16). The judgement of death was paid by Jesus who draws all men to repentance. Eternal life is the gift of God. Satan was cast from heaven no longer able to accuse the brethren before the throne of God.

> Therefore rejoice, ye heavens, and ye that dwell in them. Woe to the inhabiters of the earth and of the sea! For the devil is come down unto you, having great wrath, because he knoweth that he hath but a short time.
>
> —Revelation 12:12

Michael, the archangel, who is Jesus Christ defeated Satan on the cross. The angels in heaven rejoice because Satan has lost access to heaven to accuse the believers of God. Instead, he is bound to this earth. His fate is sealed because of his choice to rebel against God. Now Satan wages war on earth with the remnant of believers who obey the commandments of God and keep the testimony of Jesus Christ (Revelation 12:11, 14:12).

What do "woe" and the great wrath of Satan look like? Since his first temptation of man in the Garden of Eden, Satan continues to lie, deceive, and raise up powers and principalities (governments) to eliminate all godliness on earth. Satan uses all forms of vices: drugs, alcohol, abuse of food and sex, envy, bribery, jealousy, covetousness to overcome man's free will. Men become addicted and cannot make good decisions. Satan uses rebellion to bring about change and chaos to bring about his order. The Freemason motto "Order out of chaos" is nothing more than tyranny. All that Lucifer accused God of doing in heaven, he is trying to accomplish on earth through the actions of sinful man. For 6,000 years Satan has directed his anger with God toward man, and great sorrow and distress continue to affect the followers of Christ. Satan will continue his battle until Jesus returns to take His children home to heaven.

Therefore, rejoice . . . Satan's time has almost expired!

Revelation Chapter 12:1-6

The Woman and the Dragon

Revelation Chapter 12:13-17

The Dragon and the Woman

What Does This Mean?

"And he said unto them, I beheld Satan as lightning fall from heaven."

—Luke 10:18

Jesus makes this statement to his disciples about an event that has already happened. Yet, Revelation 12:9 clearly states that Satan was cast out after the resurrection of Christ. God is omniscient; He sees all eternity from beginning to end.

Jesus Christ is God in the flesh. Jesus knew that His purpose for coming to earth was to redeem man from the effects of sin. In His mind, redemption was complete; which means that Satan was already cast from heaven, and God's judgment for Satan's disobedience was complete. Therefore, Jesus could tell His disciples that He saw Satan fall from heaven.

Many future events in Revelation are written in the past tense because, in God's mind, those events are complete. In man's time, some of the events have happened, and some are still in the future. Understanding that concept will help the reader understand the events of the end time.

In prophetic terms "a woman" is a church. God describes this woman as one of great beauty and worth. Through this church came the Christ child, the Redeemer of man. Satan, the dragon, wages war against the woman.

First Chiasmus

- **Revelation 12:1**: "And there **appeared a great wonder in heaven; a woman clothed with the sun, and the moon under her feet, and upon her head a crown of twelve stars**.

- **Revelation 12:17b**: "*Which keep the commandments of God, and have the testimony of Jesus Christ.*"

John sees a great wonder in heaven. Jesus Christ describes His church using the celestial beauty of His creation. The beauty that man beholds from observing the sun, moon, stars resemble the beauty Christ beholds in the character, doctrines, and obedience of His church. She is clothed with the righteousness of Christ, which is as bright as the sun. As the moon reflects the sun, she reflects the character of Christ in her obedience to the Word of God. The number twelve symbolizes God's people, His government, and His authority. The twelve stars are her completeness in Christ for peace with God and eternal life in the kingdom of heaven. God gave His authority to His church (Matthew 28:18–20).

The true church of God keeps the commandments of God and has the testimony of Jesus Christ. The testimony of Jesus is the spirit of prophecy (Revelation 19:10). Believers in Christ are guided by the Holy Spirit to understand the deep mysteries of God. Paul told Timothy the mystery of God was manifest in the flesh as Jesus Christ. Christ was justified in the Spirit by living a sinless life. Christ was seen of angels and preached to the Gentiles or heathens. All who believe the prophecies of Jesus Christ will be justified by His atoning death on the cross and will one day be received into heaven (I Timothy 3:16). The true church will recognize the signs of the times and understand the prophecies of Jesus Christ because their focus is Christ.

Second Chiasmus

- **Revelation 12:2–5**: "And she being **with child cried, travailing in birth, and pained to be** delivered. . . . [3] and behold **a great red dragon**, having seven heads and ten horns, and seven crowns upon his heads. [4] And **his tail drew the third part of the stars of heaven, and did cast them to the earth: and the dragon stood before the woman which was ready to be delivered, for to devour her child as soon as it was born.** [5] **And she brought forth a man child, who was to rule all nations with a rod of iron: and her child was caught up unto God, and to his throne.**"

- **Revelation 12:13, 15–17a:** "And when *the dragon saw that he was cast unto the earth, he persecuted the woman which brought forth the man child.* . . . [15] And *the serpent cast out of his mouth water as a flood after the woman,* that he might cause her to be carried away of the flood. [16] And *the earth helped the woman,* and the earth opened her mouth, and swallowed up the flood which the dragon cast out of his mouth. [17a] And *the dragon was wroth with the woman and went to make war with the remnant of her seed.*"

The woman represents believers in Christ. God uses her to visit earth in human form as Immanuel, Jesus Christ.

John also sees another wonder in heaven. A great red dragon with seven heads and ten horns, and seven crowns upon his head appears in heaven. The seven crowns upon his head represent total authority over the nations or kingdoms of the earth. What has John seen? Daniel describes the same beast.

> After this I saw in the night visions, and behold a fourth beast, dreadful and terrible, and strong exceedingly; and it had great iron teeth: it devoured and brake in pieces and stamped the residue with the feet of it: and it was diverse from all the beasts that were before it; and it had ten horns.
>
> —Daniel 7:7

John and Daniel describe the Roman Empire empowered by the great red dragon, which controlled the world at the time of Jesus Christ's birth. Satan did all he could to stop the Savior's birth. When Jesus Christ was born, the wise men from the east came to Herod the king of Judea asking him, "Where is he that is born King of the Jews" (Matthew 2:2)? Herod instructed them to find the Christ child and bring him word of the child's whereabouts. God warned the wise men not to return to Herod. When Herod realized he had been mocked, he ordered every male child two years old and under to be killed. Thus, Satan tried to "devour" the Christ child.

The testimony of Jesus Christ brought by the angels overcame the great red dragon's plan. The wise men believed the warning from the angels. They obeyed God and did not return to Herod (Matthew 2:12). Joseph believed the angel's message, obeyed God, and took Mary and baby Jesus to Egypt to escape Herod's wrath (Matthew 2:13). Their faith and obedience to God protected the man child who was to rule all nations with a rod of iron. Jesus Christ will rule all nations with a rod of iron. What is the rod of iron?

- **Psalm 110:2**: "**The Lord shall send the rod of thy strength out of Zion**."

- **Psalm 23:4**: "**Thy rod and thy staff they comfort me**."

- **Psalm 89:30–32**: "If his **children forsake my law**, and walk not in my judgments; [31] If they break my statutes, and **keep not my commandments**; [32] **Then will I visit their transgression with the rod**, and their iniquity with stripes."

The man child was born to rule all nations with a rod of iron. Every kingdom has a king and laws. Jesus Christ was born to be the King of kings. His kingdom is not of this earth, but in heaven (John 18:36). Jesus is the Way into the kingdom of heaven (John 14:6). The laws of the kingdom of heaven are strong and unbending as iron. The rod is used for correction or comfort. As a shepherd uses the rod to comfort or protect his sheep inside the sheepfold; he also uses the rod to correct the sheep who wander away from the sheepfold to bring them back to safety. The rod is used to persuade those who forsake the law of God to bring them back into the will of God. The rod also comforts man giving him peace and security. The rod is the standard of God's righteousness, love, and mercy.

God's standard is his law, the Ten Commandments. Jesus Christ came to earth to fulfill the law of God (Matthew 5:17). Any man who has the faith of Christ and keeps the commandments of God is comforted by the rod because the Good Shepherd defends his faithful saints. Anyone who disobeys the law of God is an enemy of the Lawgiver and will not inherit eternal life in the kingdom of heaven.

In Revelation 12:13–17, the war over worship in heaven was brought to earth. Satan desired worship from the host of heaven, and now he desires the worship of all men. Satan infiltrated the early church with a system of worship that takes advantage of man's pride, arrogance, and his love of the world. Majestic cathedrals were built. The clergy began to dress in priestly robes. The incense of candles and the sound of beautiful music capture the senses. Religious leaders are revered with the titles of vicar, father, and holy. Worship becomes an outer display of vanity instead of an inner change of the heart. Men's ears are tickled with stories and repetitive prayers. The worshippers in the apostate church are made to feel good and worthy of heaven.

A wonderful and horrible thing is committed in the land; The prophets prophesy falsely, and their priests bear rule by their means; and my people love to have it so: and what will ye do in the end thereof?

—Jeremiah 5:30–31

"And the earth helped the woman" (Revelation 12:16). As the true church of Christ expanded and grew stronger, Satan's attacks increased. For hundreds of years throughout the Dark Ages, Christians throughout Europe who refused to follow the laws and traditions of the false church were called heretics and were severely persecuted. Many heard of a vast land across the ocean where one could worship God freely. They escaped the flood of persecution on ships headed for the new land of America. The ocean created a barrier that "swallowed up the flood" of persecutors. America offered a safe haven of religious freedom.

Third Chiasmus

- **Revelation 12:6**: "And **the woman fled into the wilderness**, where **she hath a place** prepared of God, that **they should feed her there a thousand two hundred and threescore days**."

- **Revelation 12:14**: "*And to the woman were given two wings of a great eagle*, that she might fly into the wilderness, *into her place*, where *she is nourished for a time, and times, and half a time, from the face of the serpent*."

Jesus Christ is revealing to John the "wilderness" experience of His church when she fled from the dragon. Just as the Israelites wandered throughout the wilderness, the church of God wandered for 1,260 years, hiding in caves and mountains. God provided manna and water for the Israelites. The true church in hiding was nourished on the true Word of God in their native tongue. The false church hid the Word of God, the Light of the World, from the nations during the historic Dark Ages.

During the Great Tribulation, AD 538–1798, the true church experienced the wrath of the dragon (Revelation 2:22). The doctrines of the Roman Catholic Church heavily influenced the kings and queens of Europe. During that awful period, God protected and nourished His people through His Word and the Holy Spirit. We will discuss more about this historical period in the section on the Church of Thyatira.

God protected the woman "for a time, and times, and half a time from the face of the serpent." Many verses in the book of Revelation speak of this period. Time, times, and half a time equals one thousand, two hundred sixty days or three and half years or forty-two months; these phrases are used to describe the same period in history. At the end of this time, a country rises out of the earth, which helps the woman, the true church, escape the flood of humanity seeking to destroy her. God provided deliverance for His people to the new world, which later became the United States of America, which represented the "earth" where freedom of religion and freedom of conscience were made the law of the land. The remnant of the true church continued to keep the commandments of God and to have the testimony of Jesus Christ. Truth entered the Great Tribulation, and Truth emerged from this dark period of history by the providential protection of God.

Revelation Chapter 11
The Two Witnesses

Revelation Chapter 13
The Two Beasts

What Does This Mean?

As stated in the introduction, we are presenting the book of Revelation using the chiastic structure comparing chapters and verses. We believe the Bible explains the Bible, so we quote and refer to many scriptures to explain the verses and chapters. We also believe that most of the events in the Revelation of Christ occur during the 2,000-year history of the church. When Jesus revealed the events to John, the events of the first church at Ephesus were John's present age (Revelation 2:1). Therefore, nearly every event Jesus described will occur in John's future, which for us is the church's past, present, or future. Using the Bible and history, we prayerfully interpret the events John was privileged to record. Chapters 11 and 13 describe historical events.

In Revelation Chapter 11, Jesus reveals to John the identity of the two witnesses and their journey through church history. The two witnesses testify of Jesus Christ in sackcloth and mourn the lost condition of man without the light of Jesus Christ. During this turbulent time in history, the two witnesses were removed from society. "And when they shall have finished their testimony, the beast that ascendeth out of the bottomless pit shall make war against them, and shall overcome them, and kill them" (Revelation 11:7).

In Revelation Chapter 13, Jesus describes the two beasts. A "beast" in Bible prophecy is defined as an earthly kingdom (see "Biblical Prophetic Terms"). The beasts are a system of governments with a king or leader, territory, laws, citizens, and an army to enforce laws. The first beast rises up out of the sea. In prophecy the sea or water describes people or nations (see "Biblical Prophetic Terms"). The second beast comes up out of the earth, a land of few people. Although coming from different places and at different times, these two beasts are great kingdoms on earth, which will unite to make laws that are contrary to the Law of God. Prior to the Second Coming of Christ, one such law will force all humanity to take the mark of the beast.

Chapters 11 and 13 present a mirror contrast. Who or what are the two witnesses and the two beasts?

First Chiasmus

- **Revelation 11:1–2**: "And **there was given me a reed like unto a rod:** and the angel stood, saying, **Rise, and measure the temple of God, and the altar, and them that worship therein.** ² But **the court** which is **without the temple leave out,** and **measure it not;** for **it is given unto the Gentiles.**

- **Revelation 13:1–2**: "And *I stood upon the sand of the sea,* and *saw a beast rise up out of the sea, having seven heads and ten horns,* and *upon his horns ten crowns,* and *upon his heads the name of blasphemy.* ² And the beast which I saw was like unto a leopard, and his feet were as the feet of a bear, and his mouth as the mouth of a lion: and *the dragon gave him his power, and his seat, and great authority.*

John was given a measuring rod and told to measure the temple of God, the altar, and the worshippers. To measure something is to compare it to the standard. As we stated in the previous chapter, God's standard is His immutable law. Jesus gives John the measuring rod. John and every disciple of Christ measures his faith and obedience by the rod of God's law, The Ten Commandments.

- **John 14:15**: "If you love me, keep my commandments."

- **2 Corinthians 6:16b**: "For ye are the temple of the living God."

- **Psalm 23:4b**: "For thou art with me; thy rod and thy staff they comfort me."

- **Revelation 22:14**: "Blessed are they that do his commandments, that they may have right to the tree of life, and may enter in through the gates into the city."

Every believer as "the temple of the living God" is to govern his behavior, service, and worship according to God's unchanging law.

Jesus instructs John to not measure the court, which is outside of the temple. That area is for the Gentiles who are the heathen or unbelievers (Malachi 1:11). Adulterers, murderers, idolators, those who practice witchcraft, and those who love to lie are outside the church until they choose to come in by faith in Jesus Christ (Revelation 22:15).

Jesus Christ is calling those who are outside the temple to come into the temple. Unbelievers are already condemned. They do not measure up to God's standard because they love darkness and their deeds are evil (John 3:19). God's arms are always open and ready to receive all who will repent of sin and believe in Jesus Christ. When one believes Jesus Christ is the Son of God, he will shape or mold his behavior to please God (John 3:21). A tree is known by its fruits.

In Revelation 13:1–2 John stands by the sea and sees the dreadful and terrible and exceedingly strong beast described by the prophet Daniel (Daniel 7:7). The leopard represents the kingdom of Greece with its philosophy, superstitions, gods and goddesses, temple worship, fraternal groups, and spiritualism. The bear represents the kingdom of the Medes and Persians with strict laws that even kings cannot undo. The lion represents the empire of Babylon where all apostasy originates. The dreadful beast John sees is the combination of all the previous kingdoms of the world described by Daniel.

John observes the false church of the Holy Roman Empire rising out of the sea, which is the Gentile nations of Europe. The kings of the European countries relinquished their secular authority to the religious leader of the apostate church. This false church using the laws of the Roman Empire controlled the people by fear and superstitions perverting the truth of the gospel with the traditions of men and paganism. The dragon, Satan, empowered this beastly kingdom, which combined church and state with great authority over the nations. The kings of Europe feared the leadership of the false church. The kings also feared their citizens who were bewitched by the doctrines that played upon their superstitions and ignorance of the Scriptures. Jesus Christ compares this false church to a whore. She has no values and will accommodate the beliefs of every man.

The first beast, the secular religious system, began with Roman Emperor Constantine (AD 313) during the time of the church in Pergamos (Revelation 2:12). During this time in church history, the church began to embrace blasphemous doctrines denying that Jesus Christ was the Son of God and replacing the atoning work of Christ with works of men or blessings from the church or priest. This false church evolved into the Roman Catholic Church, which ruled Europe with an iron hand for hundreds of years.

The evolution of this church strengthened during the historical period of the church at Thyatira in AD 538. Roman Emperor Justinian no longer considered himself the chief of the Roman army, but a theologian.[1] The papacy filled his vacated seat of secular authority, and the Justinian Code gave the power of the state to the false church to enforce her doctrines by severely persecuting any who would not "commit fornication" and "eat things sacrificed unto idols" (Revelation 2:20). Many Christians were persecuted for not joining the Holy Roman Catholic church, which ruled the empire. Catholic priests, including Wycliffe, Huss, Jerome, Luther, Calvin, and others protested the church's doctrine during the Reformation Period. Every reformer recognized this false church system as that of the first beast and its head the Antichrist spoken of in Revelation 13.

Second Chiasmus

- **Revelation 11:2b–5: "For it is given unto the Gentiles: and the holy city shall they tread under foot forty and two months. [3] And I will give power unto my two witnesses, and they shall prophesy a thousand two hundred and**

threescore days, clothed in sackcloth. [4] These are the two olive trees, and the two candlesticks standing before the God of the earth. [5] **And if any man will hurt them, fire proceedeth out of their mouth, and devoureth their enemies: and if any man will hurt them, he must in this manner be killed.**"

- **Revelation 13:4–5**: "And they worshipped the beast, saying, *Who is like unto the beast? Who is able to make war with him?* And there was given him a mouth speaking great things and blasphemies; *and power was given unto him to continue forty and two months.*"

Revelation 11:2–3 and Revelation 13:5 speak of the same time period. The forty-two months or 1,260 days, which are years (see "Biblical Prophetic Terms") prophesied by Daniel and confirmed by Jesus Christ to John, are the Great Tribulation period of the church. This period in history is also known as the Dark Ages or the Middle Ages. This was the zenith of Satan's war on Christ's church. Millions were slaughtered for their belief in Jesus Christ as the Son of God. (The section on the Church in Thyatira explains more about the Great Tribulation period.)

Who are the two witnesses? A witness is someone who has seen something and then relates what they have seen. The two witnesses are given authority to prophesy or foretell of an event that will last 1,260 years. The two witnesses prophesy about this event dressed in sackcloth, meaning they are in mourning clothes.

What event are they foretelling that makes them so sorrowful? The event is the slaughtering of millions of Christians for their faith during the time of the Great Tribulation when the Antichrist openly defies God. Who would have knowledge of this sorrowful event that takes place in the future? Only those who are in the presence of the Omniscient God would have access to that knowledge. Jesus reveals their identity to John.

The two witnesses are the two olive trees and the two candlesticks standing before the God of the earth.

- **Zechariah 4:14**: "Then said he, **These are the two anointed ones, that stand by the Lord of the whole earth**."

- **John 8:18**: "And the Father that sent me beareth **witness of me**."

- **John 15:26**: "But when the Comforter is come . . . **he shall testify of me**."

John states that Jesus Christ was in the beginning with God. He is the Creator of all things and the light of the world (John 1:1–4). The Word of God testifies of Jesus Christ. Jesus Christ is the Word of God. Only the Son of God, Jesus Christ, can witness of the Father.

The Apostle Peter tells us that God used "holy men," who were faithful believers in the Son of God, moved or empowered by the Holy Spirit to write the Holy Scriptures (1 Peter 1:21). The Holy Spirit of God has revealed to man everything we need to know about Him. The Holy Spirit is the only qualified One to testify of the Son of God. Jesus Christ is the only qualified One who can bear witness of Himself.

The two witnesses are Jesus Christ and the Holy Spirit. Jesus Christ is the Word of God. The church is empowered by the Holy Spirit to rightly divide, proclaim, preach, and teach the Word of Truth.

The Gentiles, the heathen unbelievers, who worship the dragon and the ungodly beast boast: "Who is like unto the beast? Who is able to make war with him?" The false church and state beast system empowered by Satan makes war against the saints of God. The apostate church speaks great blasphemies against the Word of God, Jesus Christ. Blasphemy is speaking or acting in a way that shows contempt or disrespect for God, claiming to be God, insulting God's name or character, or attributing the works of God to evil forces. The Pharisees accused Jesus Christ of blasphemy for claiming to be the "Son of man" (Matthew 26:63–64). The head of the apostate church claims to be the Vicar of Christ. This is blasphemy.

The apostate church leaders believe the lies the serpent used in the Garden of Eden (Genesis 3:1, 4, 5). The leaders doubt the authority of God's Word. They pervert God's Word with false doctrines. They believe "they are gods." The false church and her priests assume the authority of gods determining good and evil, moral and immoral. The false church and her priests judge who is righteous or unrighteous.

The apostate church has followed the great deceiver, the Dragon, Satan, and it makes war with Christ and His followers. The apostate leaders persecute those who question their false doctrines. The apostate church believes she can eliminate all heresy by burning the Scriptures and Christians at the stake.

God rewards mankind for their works (Revelation 20:13b). God took notice of the apostate church's evil actions against His people. Therefore, the fires from the trumpet judgments (Revelation 11:5) proceed from heaven during the 1,260-year period. God uses disease, famine, bitterness, condemnation, wars, and total darkness of spirit to judge the wicked. The trumpet judgments are the direct result of the apostate church's actions against God and His people.

In 1798, Pope Pius VI refused to relinquish his temporal power to Napoleon Bonaparte of France. The French government stripped Pope Pius VI of his political powers and placed him in exile where he later died. This was the head that seemed "wounded to death" (Revelation 13:3). In 1929, Italy restored the power of the papacy to Pope Pius XI, and the Vatican was again recognized as an independent sovereign state. The headline of the *San Francisco Chronicle* of February 12, 1929, stated, "Mussolini and Gasparri Sign Historic Roman Pact, Heal Wound of Many Years." The first beast's wound was healed, and "all the world wondered after the beast" (Revelation 13:3).

Third Chiasmus

- **Revelation 11:6–7, 10**: "**These have power to shut heaven,** that it rain not in the days of their prophecy: **and have power over waters to turn them to blood, and to smite the earth with all plagues,** as often as they will. ⁷ **And when they shall have finished their testimony, the beast that ascendeth out of the bottomless pit shall make war against them, and shall overcome them, and kill them.** ¹⁰ **And they that dwell upon the earth shall rejoice over them,** and make merry, and shall send gifts one to another; **because these two prophets tormented them that dwelt on the earth.**"

- **Revelation 13:6–10**: "*And he opened his mouth in blasphemy against God,* to blaspheme his name, and his tabernacle, and them that dwell in heaven. ⁷ *And it was given unto him to make war with the saints, and to overcome them:* and *power was given him* over all kindreds, and tongues, and nations. ⁸ *And all that dwell upon the earth shall worship him, whose names are not written in the book of life of the Lamb slain from the foundation of the world.* ⁹ If any man have an ear, let him hear. ¹⁰ *He that leadeth into captivity shall go into captivity: he that killeth with the sword must*

*be killed with the sword. Here is the patience
and the faith of the saints."*

The Third Chiasmus Scriptures describe the historical periods of the churches in Thyatira and Sardis (Revelation 2:18–3:6). The churches in this period experienced the Great Tribulation and the Reformation (538–1798). Revelation 13:6–7 describes the apostate church's assault on God's people. The apostate church is empowered by the dragon, Satan, and the leader of the church is the Antichrist. The Antichrist blasphemes God by placing himself and his church as the Redeemer of man. The Antichrist makes war with the saints for believing Jesus Christ is "the way, the truth, and the life" (John 14:6). Millions of Christians were imprisoned, forced to live in caves, or burned at the stake during this period.

The Great Tribulation against the true church of God continued for 1,260 years just as the Word of God foretold. God consoled the saints to persevere and keep the faith of Christ. God assured His people that their tormentors will receive the same punishment as they inflict (Revelation 13:10).

Even though the persecution of the saints was intense, the Word of God and the power of the Holy Spirit were stronger (Revelation 11:6–7). Satan did all he could to wipe Christianity off the map, but failed. Brave men began to read the Word of God and discovered that the apostate church was in error. John Wycliffe, the "Morning Star" of the Reformation translated the Bible into English. For the next 400 years, other men translated the Word into the common language of their people. Many began reading the Word of God and realized they had been deceived by the priests, and they turned to God. The Reformation Period caused much distress for the Roman Catholic Church. They were losing their grip on the people because God's truth was enlightening the hearts of believers.

During this time, many wars were fought resulting in famine and disease. Times were difficult for everyone especially the very poor. Kings and queens, the hierarchy of the church, and the leaders of the cities lived in splendor while the peasants starved. Life had become bitter for many, and they began to blame God. The dejected turned to alcohol, drugs, crime, and sexual perversions to ease their suffering. All sinful activity became their pleasure (Revelation 13:8). The huge gap between the haves and have-nots caused riots in the streets.

The climax of this period in history occurred with the riots in 1793 during the French Revolution. The people revolted against the church, the priests, and the Pope who was demanding more money for indulgences. The French Parliament, out of fear of the people arrested the Pope, banned and burned Bibles, and closed the churches (Revelation 11:7–8). God and Christians were completely removed from society. The god of Reason and Liberty was raised as the new standard of morality in France.

The people of France rejoiced and made merry and sent gifts to each other (Revelation 11:10). The people became as gods knowing good and evil. Spiritually, they were like Sodom with all sexual restraints removed and like Egypt, an atheist with no god (Revelation 11:8). Because of their rejection of Jesus Christ, their names are not written in the book of life.

Three and a half years later (Revelation 11:9), the people were tired of the lawless, Antichrist behavior. The French Parliament reversed course and allowed the Bible to be used. No more state-sponsored religion would be allowed in France.

God used this event to extend religious freedom around the world. More people from the continent of Europe were sailing to America. The Bill of Rights was written guaranteeing freedom of speech and freedom of religion. Bibles were printed in every language. Bible institutes and societies sent missionaries worldwide. The two witnesses, the Word of God empowered by the Holy Spirit, were alive and well. Great reverence and respect were given to the two witnesses (Revelation 11:11).

The Second Beast

And I beheld **another beast coming up out of the earth**; and he had two horns like a lamb, and he spake as a dragon. [12] And **he exerciseth all the power of the first beast** before him, and **causeth** the earth and them which dwell therein **to worship the first beast**, whose deadly wound was healed. [13]

And **he doeth great wonders**, so that he maketh fire come down from heaven on the earth in the sight of men, ¹⁴ And **deceiveth** them that dwell on the earth by the means of those miracles which he had power to do in the sight of the beast; saying to them that dwell on the earth, that they should **make an image to the beast**, which had the wound by a sword, and did live. ¹⁵ And **he had power to give life unto the image of the beast**, that the image of the beast should both speak and cause that as many as would not worship the image of the beast should be killed. ¹⁶ And **he causeth** all, both small and great, rich and poor, free and bond, **to receive a mark in their right hand, or in their foreheads**: ¹⁷ And that **no man might buy, or sell** save he that had the mark, or the name of the beast, or the number of his name. ¹⁸ Here is wisdom. Let him that hath understanding count the number of the beast: for it is the number of a man; and his number is Six hundred threescore and six.

—Revelation 13:11–18

Who Is the Second Beast?

John observes another beast, an earthly kingdom or government, rise as the French Revolution is ending. John describes this beast as one who comes out of the earth, which is a newly developed land of few people. The beast has two horns like a lamb, and he speaks as a dragon. This government has the characteristics of a lamb, which indicates Jesus Christ. This land accepts Christian principles.

John sees the "earth" help the church escape the oppression of the apostate church and the lawlessness of Europe (Revelation 12:16). During this historical period, many citizens of Europe fled to the new country, America. The second beast is the United States of America, the land of opportunity, free speech, and freedom of religion.

When the United States government begins to speak as a dragon, it will promote the power or doctrine of the first beast. According to Jesus Christ, this second beast will cause its citizens to worship the first beast whose deadly wound was healed. This will be accomplished by making an image to the first beast. An image is a reflection in the mirror or a photograph. When separation of church and state is removed as it was during the Dark Ages, the second beast, the United States of America, will look identical to the first beast, the Roman Catholic Church.

The United States government will give life to the first beast by promoting its doctrines and teachings. As we write this book, leaders in Washington, DC, are beginning to speak of tearing down the wall between the separation of church and state. Laws will be written and signed requiring all citizens to not only adopt the doctrines of the apostate church, but to worship the apostate church or die. These laws will affect the world. To enforce this worship, the United States government will take away people's ability to buy or sell. Tariffs and digital currencies are examples of government's ability to enforce economic restrictions.

All citizens of the world will be required to receive a mark in their right hand or in their foreheads or take the name of the beast or the number of his name which is 666. This is not a physical mark or tattoo or computer chip or credit card. In biblical prophetic terms, a mark is a sign or an identifier. Baptism identifies or marks one as a believer in Christ. A priestly robe identifies or marks the priest. Every religion has certain marks or identifiers that are applied to that belief system.

God grants freedom of conscience to every man. God wills for every man to inherit eternal life. God has qualifications for man to have the right of eternal life. God is very clear in His Word what those qualifications are. God will never force or coerce anyone to accept any belief or perform any task to inherit eternal life. God will never force anyone to worship Him. Only the beast systems force men to worship. That is why they need the mark.

What Is the Mark of the First Beast?

What is the mark or sign or identifier of worship to the image of the beast? Consider these statements from the past:

- **"The church is above the Bible**; and this trans-
  ference of Sabbath observance from Saturday to
  Sunday is proof positive of that fact."[2]

- "**Reason and sense demand** the acceptance of one or the other of these alternatives: either Protestantism and the keeping holy of Saturday or Catholicity and the keeping holy of Sunday. Compromise is impossible."[3]

- "It is well to remind the Presbyterians, Baptists, Methodists, and all other Christians, that **the Bible does not support them anywhere in their observance of Sunday. Sunday is an institution of the Roman Catholic Church**, and those who observe the day observe a commandment of the Catholic Church."[4]

The first beast, the Roman Catholic Church, will deceive all citizens across the world to break God's Law. Pope John Paul II in *Dies Domini*, 18 states, "We move from the "Sabbath" to the "first day after the Sabbath", from the seventh day to the first day: the *dies Domini* becomes the *dies Christi!*" The first beast moved God's Sabbath to Sunday, the Day of the Sun. The first beast believes their church is above the Bible and reason and sense demand all people obey them.

The second beast, the United States of America, will give the apostate church secular power through economics and the military to enforce the doctrine or the mark of the first beast. All citizens who disobey the first beast will be put to death by the second beast. Revelation 13:18 says, "Here is wisdom. Let him that hath understanding count the number of the beast: for it is the number of a man; and his number is Six hundred threescore and six."

During the height of Solomon's reign as King of Israel, all countries in the known world served or obeyed him. He controlled their economies, and the countries paid tariffs and taxes to the Kingdom of Israel.

> Now the weight of gold that came to Solomon in one year was **six hundred threescore and six talents of gold**. Beside that he had of the merchantmen, and of the traffick of the spice merchants, and of all the kings of Arabia, and of the governors of the country.
>
> —1 Kings 10:14–15

Like Solomon, these two beasts, the Roman Catholic Church and the United States of America, control the economy, banking, shipping, merchants, religions, kings, and citizens of the entire world. The countries of the world will submit to their beastly authority.

Most faithful Christians today who truly love God believe Sunday is the day of worship because Jesus rose from the grave on the first day of the week. Sunday is the only day they have ever worshipped God in church. The great deceiver, Satan, has cleverly distorted the truth from those who truly love God. The first beast clearly states in the above quotes that the Bible does not support the observance of Sunday as the day of worship. Sunday worship is the mark of their authority and a tradition of their church.

God's Law, the Ten Commandments, is His mark or seal of authority. God wrote the commandments with his finger on two tablets of stone (Exodus 31:18). The Ten Commandments were placed in the Ark of the Covenant covered by the mercy seat. Jesus Christ died on the cross of Calvary for man's disobedience to the law of God. Deuteronomy 6:8 says, "And thou shalt bind them for **a sign** upon thine hand, and they shall be as frontlets between thine eyes."

In the fourth commandment, God tells man to "**Remember the sabbath day**, to keep it holy." God set this day apart and made it holy in the Garden of Eden when God rested from His work of creation. Furthermore, in Ezekiel 20:20 God commands, "And **hallow my sabbaths**; and they shall be **a sign** between me and you, **that ye may know that I am the Lord your God**." And finally, Matthew 12:8 declares, "For the **Son of man is Lord** even **of the sabbath day**."

The day may be coming soon when man must make the choice whether to believe God's Word or the tradition of the churches.

Revelation Chapter 10
The Little Book

What Does This Mean?

The little book contains the names of those who will enter God's presence cleansed from sin, justified, and worthy of eternal life through Jesus Christ. Life is precious to God. At conception all persons are entered into the Book of Life. This book guarantees eternal life for those who overcome this sinful world with patience by keeping the commandments and the faith of Jesus (Revelation 14:12).

Jesus Christ determines whose names remain in the Book of Life. Christ enters the Most Holy Place in the sanctuary in heaven. He investigates every one's heart, motive, and life. Then Christ alone keeps the name in the Book of Life, or the name is blotted out. All sin must be confessed and covered by the atoning blood of Christ. At the Second Coming of Christ, the angels will call the names from the little book to come up to heaven. Time on earth is no more. Eternity begins.

Jesus reveals to Daniel when the little book would be opened. At the opening of that book, all time prophecies are fulfilled. The next prophecies to be watching are the signs of the times, which give clues or waymarks as to how close we are to the return of Christ.

Revelation 10 is a chiasmus unto itself and parallels with Daniel 12.

First Chiasmus: The Little Book Prophecy

- **Revelation 10:1–2:** "And **I saw another mighty angel come down from heaven**, clothed with a cloud: and a rainbow was upon his head, and his face was as it were the sun, and his feet as pillars of fire: And **he had in his hand a little book open**: and he set his right foot upon the sea, and his left foot on the earth."

- Revelation 10:6, 9: "*And sware by him that liveth for ever and ever.* . . . And *I went unto the angel, and said unto him, Give me the little book*. And he said unto me, Take it, and eat it up; and it shall make thy belly bitter, but it shall be in thy mouth sweet as honey."

- Daniel 12:7 says, "*And I heard the man clothed in linen*, which was upon the waters of the river, when he held up his right hand his left hand unto heaven, *and sware by him that liveth for ever.*"

John sees another mighty angel come down from heaven. John's description of the mighty angel is the same as he used to describe Jesus Christ in Revelation 1:13–15 and 4:3. John sees Jesus Christ just before His Second Coming in the clouds of heaven. Jesus has in His hand an open little book. John asks Jesus Christ to give the book to him. Jesus instructs John to take it and eat it. That is, John is to read the book and internalize its message. The message of the book is sweet as honey to the taste, but will make the belly bitter. The message is sweet, but will have bitter consequences. The vision recorded by the prophet Daniel is the same vision as the one recorded by John.

Both John and Daniel see Jesus Christ with the little book. Daniel sees Christ as Michael, the great prince, the Savior and Mediator between man and God. Jesus shows Daniel that there shall be a time of great trouble in the future for the people of God. At that time of great trouble, every name found written in the book will be delivered or saved. All the dead who sleep in the dust of the earth will at some future day be resurrected. Those who are saved will be awakened in the first resurrection to everlasting life and will live and reign with Christ (Revelation 20:6). The unrepentant will awake one thousand years later to shame and everlasting contempt because of their unbelief and disobedience to God. They will be cast into the lake of fire which is the second death (Revelation 20:14).

John sees Christ with the little book in his hand prior to His Second Coming. John is to tell the church to prepare and look for the Second Coming of Christ. The hope of resurrection and eternal life is the sweet message for all who believe in Jesus Christ as their Savior. For believers, the thought of family and friends who reject the message of redemption is very bitter. Only God will be able to wash away all the tears of sadness (Revelation 21:4).

Second Chiasmus: End of Time Prophecy

- **Revelation 10:4–6: "Seal up those things** which the seven thunders uttered, and **write them not . . . that there should be time no longer:"**

- **Revelation 10:7–8:** "But in the days of the voice of the seventh angel, when he shall begin to sound, *the mystery of God should be finished. . . . Go and take the little book which is open in the hand of the angel."*

But thou, O Daniel, shut up the words, and **seal the book,** even **to the time of the end:** many shall run to and fro, and **knowledge shall be increased. . . .** sware by him that liveth for ever that it shall be for a time, times, and an half . . . **all these things shall be finished.**

—Daniel 12:4, 7

John and Daniel received the same vision of Jesus Christ holding a book. They were both told to seal the book until the

time of the end when there shall be "time no longer." Jesus
Christ tells John the end of time will come in the days when
the seventh angel begins to sound. At that time the mystery
of God, which He had declared to the prophets, should be
finished. Jesus revealed to Daniel that days, or an amount of
time, "time, times, and an half" would be involved for the
mystery of God to be finished. What is this amount of time
for the mystery of God to be finished? Daniel's prophecy
contains the answer.

During Jesus's crucifixion week, his disciples asked him
three questions in Matthew 24:3: "Tell us, **when shall these
things be?** and **what shall be the sign of thy coming**, and
of the end of the world?"

Their first question dealt with the Temple being destroyed
in Jerusalem. The Roman army totally destroyed Herod's
Temple in Jerusalem in AD 70. Many of the disciples lived
to see the fulfillment of that prophecy. The next two questions were about the Second Coming of Jesus Christ. Jesus
began to tell them the conditions of the world from the time
He would ascend into heaven until His Second Coming.
Then he instructed them to read and understand the Prophet
Daniel as He referenced the "**abomination of desolation**,
spoken of by Daniel the prophet" (Matthew 24:15).

God revealed to Daniel the time of the abomination or
transgression of desolation. Abomination is idolatry, worshipping anything or anyone in place of God the Creator.
Idol worship leads to desolation, destruction. The Old Testament records the relationship God had with his people,

Israel. The nation Israel rejected God time and again, and the kings of Israel and Judah led the people into idolatry. God sent prophets to plead for his people to return to Him, and He would forgive their sin of idolatry. But Israel and Judah continued to reject God. As a result, the northern tribes of Israel were overtaken by the Assyrians and scattered throughout the Assyrian kingdom. Years later, the tribe of Judah was overtaken by the Babylonian Empire. Solomon's Temple in Jerusalem was completely destroyed. The Hebrews became slaves to Nebuchadnezzar; the house of Israel was desolate and was scattered throughout the world.

Daniel was greatly loved by God (Daniel 9:23). He lived most of his life in the Babylonian Empire after the captivity of Judah. During the seventy years of captivity, Daniel remained faithful to God. God revealed to Daniel the kingdoms that would dominate the earth from the time of Babylon until the Second Coming of Jesus Christ. God also revealed to Daniel prophecies of time when major events would occur. Both Hebrews and Gentiles would be affected by these major events.

Daniel recorded three, time prophecies that stretched a total of 2,300 years in the book of Daniel chapters 8, 9, and 12. Jesus referred his disciples to the time prophecies of Daniel. Consider this exchange from Daniel 8:13–14: "**How long shall be the vision concerning** the daily sacrifice, and **the transgression of desolation**. . . . And he said unto me, **Unto two thousand and three hundred days;** then shall the sanctuary be cleansed."

God revealed to Daniel that the seventh angel would begin to sound at the end of 2,300 years, signaling the end of time and the fulfillment of the mystery of God (Daniel 7:9–14). As in the Day of Atonement (Leviticus 16), Jesus Christ as our High Priest enters into the Most Holy Place in the sanctuary in heaven. The books are opened. He cleanses the altar of the record of sin, the transgression of desolation. How do sins get into the heavenly sanctuary?

God instructed Moses concerning the sacrificial system of worship. When an individual sinned, he was required to bring a lamb to the temple as an atonement for his sin. Without the shedding of blood, there is no remission of sin (Hebrews 9:22). The guilty would place his hand on the head of the lamb, confess his sin, thereby transferring the guilt of sin onto the innocent lamb. The lamb would then be killed, and its blood was collected into a bowl. The Priest would enter the sanctuary and place a drop of blood on the altar of incense. On the Day of Atonement, the High Priest entered the Holy of Holies and purged or cleansed the altar of the sin record.

The earthly sanctuary was but an example, a picture, of the heavenly sanctuary. All prayers of the saints (Revelation 8:4), including confessions of sin are placed on the altar of incense. The sin record must be purged or cleansed from the heavenly sanctuary. Jesus began cleansing the sanctuary at the end of the 2,300-year prophecy.

Since 1844 Jesus Christ has been in the sanctuary of the Temple in heaven cleansing and justifying the names in the Book of Life (Daniel 8:14). Christ stands as the Mediator, the High Priest, and the Judge of man. Every name will be inspected. Every man makes the choice to believe or disbelieve God's Word. Those who have no faith in Christ and disobey His commandments will be blotted out of the Book of Life. Those who keep the commandments of God and the faith of Jesus (Revelation 14:12) will not be blotted out of the Book of Life. Sins of the redeemed are cast as far as the east is from the west and are never remembered (Psalm 103:12, Hebrews 8:12).

In prophecy a day is a year. The 2,300-year prophecy began during the Kingdom of the Medes and Persians. The start date was 457 BC, and it ended in 1844. The prophet Daniel was praying to be shown when the Babylonian Captivity would end, and he was seeking to know the beginning of the 2300-year prophecy (Daniel 9). Daniel believed that when one time prophecy ended, the other one began. God sent Gabriel to make the vision of the 2,300-year prophecy known to Daniel. Gabriel informed Daniel that the beginning dates to both the 2,300-year prophecy and the 70-week prophecy are the same. The first 490 years of the prophecy are reserved for Daniel's people. The remaining 1,810 years include all the time prophecies made to Daniel. At the end of the 2,300 years, the cleansing of the sanctuary in heaven begins and all of the time prophecies are ceased. In 457 BC Artaxerxes, King of Persia, allowed Ezra to return to Jerusalem to rebuild the Temple (Ezra 7). The time prophecy concerning the coming of the Messiah also began in 457 BC and ended 70 weeks (490 years) later in AD 34 (Daniel 9:24–27).

Included in the 2,300-year prophecy is the time (1 year), times (2 years), and a half (1/2 year) period (Daniel 12:7). This 1,260-year prophecy covered the Dark Ages of history (AD 538–1798). Daniel saw that three kings must be removed before the 1,260-year prophecy could begin (Daniel 7:8). The 1,260-year prophecy began in AD 538 when Emperors Zeno and Justinian of the Byzantine Empire overthrew the kings of the Heruli, Vandals, and Ostrogoths. The king of the Ostrogoths was the last to be removed in AD 538. That same year, Emperor Justinian stepped down as the leader of the army of the Roman Empire and assumed the clergy of the Roman church. In AD 538 the Holy Roman Empire was created, and the prophetic clock of Daniel began to tick.

The 1,290-year prophecy (Daniel 12:11) began in 508 when King Clovis of France unified Europe to Catholicism with the Pope as the head of church and state. This prophecy ended in 1798 during the French Revolution. Also, the 1,335-year prophecy (Daniel 12:12) began in 508 and ended in 1843. All of Daniel's prophecies of time have been fulfilled:

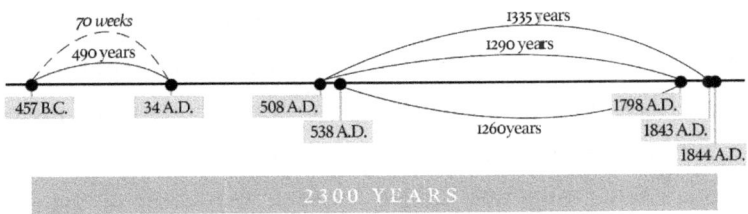

70 weeks
490 years
1335 years
1290 years
457 B.C. 34 A.D. 508 A.D. 538 A.D. 1260 years 1798 A.D. 1843 A.D. 1844 A.D.
2300 YEARS

God's prophetic calendar began in 457 BC and continued for 2,300 years until 1844 when there shall be time no longer (Revelation 10:6). All prophecies of time are now fulfilled.

Jesus Christ does not need hundreds of years to inspect the record of man. So why take so long? Because of God's great love and mercy for man. Genesis 6 records the story of Noah and of God's great judgment on man. God saw that every imagination of the thoughts of man's heart was only evil continually. It grieved God to destroy His creation with a flood. Noah found grace in God's eyes. For 120 years Noah preached the love, grace, and mercy of God. Noah warned unrepentant man of the coming judgment of God. They mocked God and scoffed at Noah's message.

One day, God instructed Noah and his family to load the ark. Eight souls out of the millions on earth boarded the ark. For seven more days nothing happened. Why? To prove the unbelievers and the believers. God's love, grace, and mercy continued to extend to the unbeliever. God desired that none perish, but that all would repent. They could have repented, believed God, and boarded the ark with Noah and the seven others. God also proved Noah and his family. For seven days, they continued to believe and obey God even though no rain drops fell. No one knew when the flood would begin. After seven days, God shut the door. The unbelievers faced judgment, and Noah and his family experienced deliverance by God. Each group was judged by their works, or choice, to believe or disbelieve God.

The Church of Laodicea represents the church of today. Christians are neither hot or cold. Many do not believe or obey God. Many doubt the Second Coming of Christ. Many believe they will not face any tribulation or persecutions, so there is no need to worry about obeying God. Many are unprepared for His return and will be caught off guard at His appearing like a thief in the night (Matthew 24:43). God in His great love, grace, and mercy for man is longsuffering. But He will not wait forever. The prayers of the saints who were slain for their faith cry out to their Heavenly Father. He hears them and will one day, maybe soon, send Jesus Christ back to gather His children. No one knows when that day will come.

No longer are the books sealed; they have been opened because we are in the time of the end. Knowledge has increased (Daniel 12:4). Everyone has access to the Bible and a vast supply of knowledge on their smart phone. Missionaries have circled the globe preaching Christ the Redeemer of man. The time to prophesy or preach Jesus Christ is now. The signs of the times reveal His Second Coming is soon.

Revelation Chapter 7
The 144,000

Revelation Chapter 14
The Three Angels' Message

What Does This Mean?

"And he said unto me, Thou must prophesy again before many peoples, and nations, and tongues, and kings."

—Revelation 10:11

The 144,000 are saints of God living during the last days of time on earth. These faithful saints from all over the world will fulfill this prophecy of Jesus Christ by proclaiming the message of the three angels. They will preach redemption, obedience to God, and the Second Coming of Christ. The

144,000 will stand for Christ with the rod of iron, his law. They will preach in opposition to the whore of Babylon calling believers of Christ to come out of her. They will caution all people not to accept the mark of the beast or worship the image of the beast. For their testimony of Christ, these saints will be severely persecuted. Their prophecy or preaching is God's last message of redemption to man. Who are the 144,000, and when do they preach?

First Chiasmus

Revelation 7 and 14 complement each other.

- **Revelation 7:2**: "And he **cried with a loud voice** to the four angels, to whom it was given to hurt the earth and the sea."

- **Revelation 14:2**: "And *I heard a voice from heaven, as the voice of many waters, and as the voice of a great thunder*: and I heard the voice of harpers harping with their harps:"

John sees four angels holding the four winds of the earth. In prophecy, winds signify war. God instructs the angels to hold back worldwide war until the servants of God have been sealed. John also hears a great voice from heaven; this is the same voice of thunder that John heard in Revelation 10:4–7. John sees the time when "the mystery of God should be finished" and "there should be time no longer."

John also hears Jesus instruct the angels to wait until all God's servants are sealed in their foreheads. The worldwide wars are not allowed to begin until the servants of God are sealed. As in the days of rebellious Israel before Nebuchadnezzar destroyed Jerusalem, God sent his prophet Ezekiel with a message to "set a mark upon the foreheads of the men that sigh and that cry for all the abominations that be done in the midst thereof" (Ezekiel 9:4).

God has always had a remnant of people who love and obey Him. Many in Jerusalem had rejected God. The land was "full of blood, and the city full of perverseness" and the wicked were so bold in their actions that they believed, "The Lord hath forsaken the earth, and the Lord seeth not" (Ezekiel 9:9). Today, the whole earth is full of killing and all manner of perverseness. The wicked are bold in believing that there is no God to see their wicked ways. In this world of wicked abominations, saints of God stand pure as "virgins." They "follow the Lamb," Jesus Christ. They are the "redeemed . . . and are without fault before the throne of God" (Revelation 14:4-5). They are the 144,000 whom God will preserve.

Second Chiasmus

- **Revelation 7:4**: "And **I heard the number of them which were sealed: and there were sealed an hundred and forty and four thousand** of all the tribes of the children of Israel."

- **Revelation 14:1**: "And I looked and, lo, a Lamb stood on the mount Sion, and *with him an hundred forty and four thousand*, having his Father's name written in their foreheads."

Who are the sealed 144,000? Jesus identifies them in Revelation 14:4–5:

- The 144,000 are not defiled with women, for they are virgins. They are believers in Christ who "search the scriptures" (John 5:39). They believe the truth of God's Word.

- The 144,000 follow the Lamb wherever He goes. They follow Christ, their Savior. "If any man will come after me, let him deny himself, and take up his cross, and follow me" (Matthew 16:24).

- The 144,000 are redeemed from among men. They are the "whosoevers" (John 3:16) who believe in the name of Jesus Christ and are redeemed.

- The 144,000 are the firstfruits of God and the Lamb. They are dedicated to God in their lives, in worship, and in obedience. They acknowledge that Jesus Christ alone is worthy of worship and that all blessings come from God the Father.

- The 144,000 are the ones who speak no guile. No cunning or deception is found in them.

They speak the truth of God's Word. They have integrity.

- The 144,000 are without fault before the throne of God. They are justified before God because they have trusted in the blood of Jesus Christ to cleanse them from their sins.

The 144,000 are those who in the last days before Christ's second appearing live faultless lives before God and man embracing the Word of God, having the faith of Jesus Christ, and keeping the commandments of God (Revelation 14:12). They are God's faithful saints from all over the world who live to see the return of Christ. Jesus tells John that these people have a new song to sing that no one can sing but them.

In Revelation 15:3 Jesus tells John that just as Moses sang a song in the wilderness, the 144,000 will sing "the song of the Lamb." A song is a lived experience. Deuteronomy 32 is the song of Moses. Moses was the man God chose to lead His people out of Egypt to the Promised Land. Jesus Christ, the Lamb of God, was the only One who could redeem man. None other could do the work of Moses or Jesus. Moses, the man of God, and Jesus Christ, the son of God, lived unique experiences. The 144,000 will live a unique experience. They will be the generation of believers to live through the very last days of trouble on earth. They will see their Savior descend from heaven on a cloud.

Jesus not only gave John the number of 144,000, but

also told him that 12,000 would come from all the tribes of the children of Israel. In the Old Testament, the names of sons had special meanings to describe their character. Jacob's name meant "trickster." After Jacob wrestled with God all night to receive his blessing to safely enter the land of his father, God renamed him Israel (Genesis 32:28). The name Israel means "prince of God" or "overcomer." Paul taught the members in the churches of Galatia that Christians in the true church today are the "Israel of God" (Galatians 6:16).

Jesus makes many promises to the overcomers in the churches (Revelation 2 and 3). Jacob overcame his doubt, fear, and sin by obeying God and not letting go until God blessed him. Believers today overcome doubt, fear, and sin by obeying God and not letting go of faith until they enter the land of the Heavenly Father (Revelation 12:11).

The sons of Israel were given names that had special meanings, which are recorded in Genesis 29 and 30. Listed below are the names of each tribe with the meaning of their name.

- Judah: Now I will praise the Lord.
- Reuben: Surely the Lord hath looked upon my affliction.
- Gad: A troop cometh.
- Asher: Will call me blessed.
- Naphtali: I have prevailed.
- Manasseh: For God hath made me forget all my toil.

- Simeon: The Lord hath heard I was hated.

- Levi: My husband will be joined unto me.

- Issachar: God hath given me my hire.

- Zabulon: Now will my husband dwell with me.

- Joseph: God hath taken away my reproach.

- Benjamin: Son of the right hand.

The meanings of these names describe the testimony or the song of the 144,000 witnesses during the last days before the Lord returns. The 144,000 witnesses on earth will praise the Lord during their affliction when they are the troop being persecuted for Christ. They will be called blessed because they have prevailed and kept the testimony of Christ. God will make them forget all their toil because they were hated. The faithful bride of Christ will be joined to her husband and will be given eternal life to dwell with Him forever. God has taken away their reproach and they are the son of His right hand. This will be their song of praise to God.

The three angels reveal to John the message of the 144,000.

First Angel's Message

"Having **the everlasting gospel to preach unto them that dwell on the earth,** and to every nation, and kindred, and tongue, and people. [7] Saying with a loud voice, **Fear God, and give glory to him**; for the hour of his judgment is come: and **worship him that made heaven, and earth, and the sea, and the fountains of waters."**

—Revelation 14:6–7

"What doth the Lord thy God require of thee, but *to fear the Lord thy God*, . . . [13] *To keep the commandments of the Lord.*"

—Deuteronomy 10:12–13

"For in six days *the Lord made heaven and earth, the sea, and all that in them is, and rested the seventh day*: wherefore the Lord blessed the sabbath day, and hallowed it."

—Exodus 20:11

John sees another angel flying in the midst of heaven having the everlasting gospel to preach to all who dwell on earth. The everlasting gospel reverences God and gives glory to Him. Every man fears the Lord by obeying His commandments and laws, loving Him, and serving God with all of one's heart and soul (Matthew 22:36–40). God, as the Creator of all things, is worthy of man's reverence and worship.

The first angel also announces that the hour of God's judgment is come. John saw the beginning of that hour in Revelation 10:1–3. The little book, which is the Book of Life, is now opened. Jesus Christ is in the Holy Place in Heaven judging humanity. The names of those who fear God and give glory to Him by worshipping Him and keeping His commandments remain in the Book of Life. The names of those who blaspheme God, do not give Him glory or worship, and reject His commandments are blotted out of the Book of Life.

Jesus Christ gave the little book to John (Revelation 10:10). Every man is given the invitation to eat as John ate the little book. To eat the book is to internalize the message of the everlasting gospel. Every man decides for himself if the gospel message is sweet as honey or bitter to the belly. The first angel's message is God's invitation of redemption to man. God is pleading with every man to come. Even though one may be a great sinner, God's grace and mercy is available to all. The blood of Christ can cleanse anyone who repents and turns to God (Isaiah 1:18).

The message the 144,000 preach in the last days is to fear God, give glory to Him, and worship God the Creator. Worship is the expression of reverence and adoration for God. The Lord is His name. The Creator is His title. Heaven and earth are His dominion. The Lord thy God is to be worshipped because He is the Creator of all things. After God completed His last act of creation making man in His image, He rested on the seventh day, the Sabbath. God blessed and sanctified the seventh day as the day of rest and worship in the Garden of Eden (Genesis 2:3). God gave Moses the Ten Commandments on Mount Sinai (Exodus 20). God's fourth commandment instructs His people to remember that He is the God of creation and the God of salvation. God is the only one who gives man physical and eternal life. God is worthy of worship on His day.

Second Angel's Message

> **"Babylon is fallen, is fallen**, that great city, because **she made all nations drink of the wine of the wrath of her fornication."**
>
> —Revelation 14:8

> *"Babylon the great is fallen, is fallen, ... For all nations have drunk of the wine of the wrath of her fornication."*
>
> —Revelation 18: 2–3

In the time of Ezekiel, the city of Jerusalem was guilty of the same abominations as the end time apostate church of Babylon. In Chapter 8 of the book of Ezekiel, God gave Ezekiel a vision of Jerusalem's idolatry. She, like Babylon, was drunk on the doctrine of the pagan nations. She had accepted image worship on the altar. The apostate church Babylon erects many images such as the cross, saints, prayer gardens. Babylon has removed God's second commandment to justify her image worship.

The priests in the temple of God in Jerusalem had polluted the house of God. Their abominable acts were done under the cloak of darkness. Every man was doing what was right in his own eyes. Acceptable worship and atonement for sins was determined by their word. They became so vain in their actions that they believed the God of heaven could not see them and that He had forsaken them.

The priests of Babylon in the apostate church are guilty of the same abominations at the end of time. Scandals done under the cover of darkness in secret have come to light. Secret meetings and societies infiltrate schools, universities, governments, and industry with heretical teachings to unify everyone under one ecumenical movement. Secret conclaves decide who will be worshipped, canonized into sainthood, and what laws are to be obeyed. Babylon is so vain that she believes her leader is infallible and that her traditions are higher than the Word of God.

Both Jerusalem and Babylon commit "greater abominations." Jerusalem replaced the promised Messiah with Tammuz (Ezekiel 8:13–14). Babylon, the apostate church, replaces the Savior Jesus Christ with treasures of merit. Paul clearly stated to the church at Ephesus that it is the grace of God that saves man through man's faith in the blood of Jesus Christ. Sinful man does not have any merit to work his way to heaven (Ephesians 2:8–9).

God reveals even "greater abominations" committed by both Jerusalem and Babylon (Ezekiel 8:15–16). The princes or rulers of Jerusalem sit in Moses's seat and assume great authority (Matthew 23:2). They turn their backs toward the temple of the Lord, face toward the east, and worship the sun. The priests are teaching the people to worship the creation rather than the Creator, an abominable heresy.

Roman Emperor Constantine instituted the "Venerable Day of the Sun" in 321 to worship the Roman sun god, Sol Invictus meaning "unconquered Sun." Sol Invictus symbolized the sun's power as a life-giving force, strength, eternity, and the triumph of light over darkness. Constantine's motive was to combine Roman paganism with Judaism and Christianity into one ecumenical group. Emperor Constantine was part of the Solis Invictus cult. Through syncretism, the joining together of religious groups into one, Constantine chose Sunday as the day of worship because of his pagan cult belief. He issued an edict on March 7, 321: "On the venerable day of the sun let the magistrates and people residing in cities rest, and let all workshops be closed. In the country, however, persons engaged in agriculture may freely and lawfully continue their pursuits."[5]

Jerusalem could not be reformed, and neither can the apostate church of Babylon. Pope John Paul II in *Dies Domini 27* May 31, 1998 states, "Wise pastoral intuition suggested to the Church the christianization of the notion of Sunday as 'the day of the sun.' This was in order to draw the faithful away from the seduction of cults which worshipped the sun." The Sol Invictus cult that met on Sunday was legislated by Constantine as the day of worship. The Roman Catholic Church decided to christianize Sunday to follow the law of Constantine. Therefore, Sunday continues to be the day of worship for most religions. "Pastoral intuition" chose the first day, Sunday, as the day to worship God. God chose the seventh day, sabbath, as his day of worship. God told Ezekiel that Jerusalem was going to be judged for her sun worship. Jesus told John that Babylon is fallen because of her cult worship.

> "Therefore will I also deal in fury: mine eye shall not spare, neither will I have pity: and though they cry in mine ears with a loud voice, yet will I not hear them."
>
> —Ezekiel 8:18

Most believers in all faiths have no idea of the history of Sunday worship. Many believe we worship on Sunday since Christ rose on the first day of the week. We inherited this lie. A careful reading of the book of Acts reveals the first church at Jerusalem and the apostles continued to worship God on the sabbath, not the first day of the week. Secular history records the beginning of Sunday worship with Constantine.

> **"Come out of her, my people** . . . and that ye receive not of her plagues."
>
> —Revelation 18:4

God is giving mankind the last plea to "Repent, for the kingdom of heaven is at hand" (Matthew 3:2; 4:17).

Third Angel's Message:

"If any man worship the beast and his image, and receive his mark in his forehead, or in his hand, The same shall drink of the wine of the wrath of God, which is poured out without mixture into the cup of his indignation; . . . "

—Revelation 14:9–10

John hears the third angel cry with a loud voice. The angel's message is one of decision. If anyone chooses to worship the beast and his image (false religious system) and receives his mark (identification with that system) in his forehead (knowledge) or in his hand (action), that person will experience the wrath of God. In the false religious beast system, the mark of obedience is **either** knowledge **or** works. God's mark is knowledge **and** works: faith and obedience.

A mark is an identifier or sign that indicates one's beliefs. A Christian is one who identifies himself with Christ through faith. The mark, or the identifier, of a Christian is a life lived by obedience to God. In contrast, those who have no faith in God are marked by their actions of sin and disobedience to God. Only omniscient God knows the heart of man.

The day is quickly approaching when mankind must make a decision to believe and submit to God. Many desire to have the name of Christ, "Christian," but do not submit to His authority in their lives. Faith in Jesus Christ and obedience to God separate the goats from the sheep, the wheat from the tares (Matthew 13:30, 25:32). Man's actions mark or signal the belief of the heart.

The wrath of God is poured out because of an unrepentant heart. This strange work of God that brings absolute destruction goes against His character of love and mercy (Isaiah 28:21). God is the Creator, not a destroyer. He desires that none perish but that all have eternal life. His wrath comes because God cannot be in the presence of sin. Therefore, the sinner who hides his sins under the rocks and in the mountain (Revelation 6:16) will receive God's wrath because he refuses to humble himself, admit he is a sinner, and repent. The sinner is not fireproof (Hebrews 12:29, Isaiah 43:2). God is Holy. Sinful man cannot stand in the presence of God because He is a consuming fire. Man must be clothed in the righteousness of Christ so that he will not be consumed in His presence. All men must heed the message of the three angels preached by the 144,000.

Revelation Chapter 8
The Seven Trumpets

Revelation Chapter 15
The Seven Angels

What Does This Mean?

The Bible is filled with events of man's rebellion against God. Numbers 16 records the rebellion of Korah against God's servant, Moses. God chose Moses to be the leader of the Israelites, but Korah thought he could do a better job. Korah instigated an insurrection against Moses. Korah's actions questioned God's authority. The Israelites had divided into two camps: one that believed in God's authority and one that did not.

Jesus Christ commissioned His church to go into all the world teaching and preaching the gospel (Matthew 28:19–20). Soon after His resurrection, many like Korah began to question the authority of the church to teach and preach the gospel. Soon, the true church of God was perverted with paganism and false doctrines. The people were again divided into two camps: one that believed in God's authority and one that did not.

Satan mars God's perfect creation with sin. His hatred for God extends to all God's creation. Satan sows the seed of rebellion in man's heart. God is not a destroyer; Satan is the destroyer; sin destroys. God is not in heaven thinking of ways to hurt man. Man's sinful actions hurt man. Hate, envy, and greed lead to misunderstandings, which lead to wars, which cause famine, which cause disease, which cause death.

The trumpet judgments are the consequence of man's sinful actions against God's creation. God uses these events to lead man to reevaluate his actions. Just as Korah's rebellion caused a plague, man's sinful actions cause war, famine, and disease. People will again divide into two camps: believers looking to God and unbelievers blaming God.

Numbers 16:48 says, "And he stood between the dead and living; and the plague was stayed." Korah and those who followed him had many opportunities to repent. Moses prayed for them. The atonement testified of God's love and mercy for them. Korah and his followers refused to repent, accept God's mercy, and submit to His authority. Therefore, they experienced God's wrath. They died in the plague because of their choice to deny God.

Any group or organization or government that hinders or changes the gospel of Jesus Christ will also face the wrath of

God. Throughout the history of the church, God has poured out his wrath mixed with mercy to persuade men to trust and believe in Jesus Christ.

Since Christ returned to heaven, man has experienced wars, famines, diseases, and earthquakes in many places (Matthew 24:7). Christians and the earth groan under the weight of sin and prayerfully anticipate His return (Revelation 6:10). Six of the seven trumpets have sounded.

The trumpet judgments are like mile markers on the highway. The judgments identify to the faithful student of God's Word where man is on God's timeline. The judgments are assurance to the saved child of God that He is in control and that His word is sure. The judgments are a caution to the unsaved to persuade them to believe that God is in control and that His word is true.

The seven angels will pour out the last seven vials of plagues without mercy when the four winds are released (Revelation 7:1).

First Chiasmus

- **Revelation 8:2–4**: "And **I saw the seven angels which stood before God**; and to them were given seven trumpets. ³ And **another angel came and stood at the altar, having a golden censer; and there was given unto him much incense, that he should offer it with the prayers of all saints upon the golden altar which was before the** throne. *⁴ **And the smoke of the incense**, which came with the prayers of the saints, ascended up before God out of the angel's hand."

- **Revelation 15:1, 8**: "And *I saw another sign in heaven, great and marvelous, seven angels having the seven last plagues*; for in them is filled up the wrath of God. . . . *⁸ And the temple was filled with smoke from the glory of God, and from his power; and no man was able to enter into the temple*, till the seven plagues of the seven angels were fulfilled."

John sees seven angels standing before God, and they were given seven trumpets. In prophecy, trumpets are used to sound the alarm. John also sees another angel standing at the altar with a golden censer full of incense. These are the prayers of all saints offered upon the altar before the throne of God (Revelation 6:9–11). These saints asked God how long it will be until their blood is avenged. The sounding of the trumpet judgments is the avenging of their blood. The trumpet judgments were poured out in mercy.

John sees another sign in heaven. Seven angels have the seven last plagues filled up with the wrath of God. Again, the temple is filled with the smoke of the prayers of the saints giving God glory. These are the saints who have the testimony of Jesus Christ and have kept His commandments. These are the saints living in the last days of earth who have not taken the mark of the beast or worshipped his image. They cry to the Lord asking how long they must endure until He returns. The answer is until the seven last plagues are fulfilled without mercy to the unrighteous.

Christ warned His disciples of the signs of the end times. Every generation of saints since Jesus Christ has heard the trumpet sounds of war and rumors of wars, famines, pestilences, and earthquakes. Jesus admonished His disciples to not be deceived (Matthew 24). Paul instructed the members of the church at Ephesus to put on the armor of God and get ready to fight the battle with Satan because he would surely attack (Ephesians 6). Satan continues to attack the believers of God. The time has come for God to answer the prayers of believers. How long before His return? How much worse can things become?

The trumpet judgments are against those who have for centuries abused and oppressed God's faithful servants. The final vial judgments will not affect God's people, only unbelievers. As the Israelites were not affected by the final plagues in Egypt, so God will protect the sealed believers on earth during this fearful, terrible "time of trouble" (Daniel 12:1). During the last days the sealed of God on earth will endure the harshness of unbelievers, witness God's grace and mercy, and proclaim His salvation to unbelievers until they hear the last trump sound.

Revelation Chapters 8 and 9
The Seven Trumpets Sound

Revelation Chapter 16
The Seven Vials Poured Out

What Does This Mean?

These chapters are a mirror image of God's dealing with sinful man. At the sound of the trumpet, God gives a warning to humanity to repent. The trumpets have sounded throughout the history of the church. The vial judgments poured out on the earth are God's final act of judgment on His creation. Sinful mankind is judged "according to their works" (Revelation 20:12).

A word about the judgment of God is needed. God is **love**. God is long-suffering with man "not willing that any should perish, but that all should come to repentance" (2 Peter3:9). God so loved all of mankind that He sent Jesus to pay the penalty of sin, which is death (John 3:16). At the cross, Christ satisfied God's penalty for sin. Jesus Christ's resurrection defeated Satan. Man should no longer live under the curse of sin; he can have the freedom of peace with God through the sacrifice of Jesus Christ. Every man must make the choice whether to accept God's offer of grace and free pardon of sin.

Every man will be judged by God according to the Word of God, the testimony of Jesus Christ. The saints of God receive the testimony of Christ gladly and are sealed with forgiveness by His blood. The unrepentant, unbelieving mockers of God are judged according to their works. The consequences of their sinful actions will cause their destruction. Lost, unrepentant man removes himself from the protection of the loving Heavenly Father.

The trumpet judgments of Revelation 8 and 9 are God's signal to his people throughout the history of the church. The trumpets began to blow during the first century of church history, and the final trump will sound at the coming of Christ in the air to gather His people from earth. In the Old Testament, the priests sounded the trumpets to gather the people for worship, for celebrations, or as a warning of approaching danger. God uses the trumpet judgments to remind His people of His love, protection, and provision. The events and consequences of the judgments are recorded in history. Six of the trumpets have sounded, warning mankind "to repent for the kingdom of heaven is at hand" (Matthew 3:2). The return of Jesus Christ is quickly approaching. God's people are called to hold fast to the testimony of Jesus Christ and keep the commandments of God.

God's method of dealing with His people has never changed. In the Old Testament, God called Abraham to be the father of many nations. One of those nations, Israel, would represent God and proclaim His glory to those on earth. Israel was to be the witness of God's love, mercy, protection, and provision for His people. God protected His people while they were in captivity in Egypt. God used Moses to lead His people out of the land of bondage in Egypt to a land of promise. After Israel had settled in the promised land, they continued to disobey God and longed for the false gods of Egypt. Man's tendency is to worship what he can see, feel, handle, and manipulate. Faith in the unseen God is difficult. Faith requires humbly surrendering yourself to the unseen power of God. God continued to warn and plead with His people to turn from their wicked ways back to Him. When they persisted in putting their faith in the gods of wicked nations such as Egypt or Assyria, their misguided choices caused unwanted consequences. Plagues, famines, wars, and captivity were the result. God hates sin, and He will cleanse His creation from its harmful effects.

Simply put: God uses "natural" disasters and "man-made" disasters to gain the attention of man. As I write this chapter, California wildfires are raging. God did not cause those fires. The fires give Him no pleasure. The fires destroy the landscape of His creation, and more importantly they destroy people whom He loves. But through the fires, His message is proclaimed. The people who believe in God see His protection and have hope to rebuild their lives. Those who believe in their wealth, skill, or government become bitter and hopeless. The same fire event happened to both groups of people, but with different results. Hopefully, unbelievers will hear the message of hope and change their minds. That is the point of the trumpet judgments. Change your mind and your heart and believe God loves you. Humble yourself before God, repent, and trust Him for forgiveness. Then live a life that can overcome every obstacle because of God's strength, power, love, mercy, and grace.

The vial judgments will be poured out in rapid succession upon the unrepentant wicked prior to the return of Jesus Christ. The vial judgments reward the wicked for their evil actions and are the final act of God cleansing His creation. Revelation 18:8 says, "Therefore shall her plagues come in **one day**, death, and mourning and famine; and she shall be utterly burned with fire: for strong is the Lord God who judgeth her."

According to Jesus Christ, these plagues come in one day. In prophecy, one day is one year. No one knows for certain what the vial judgments will be or when that one day will come. We can only use the Word of God and history to imagine the scenes John the Revelator was describing. The Word of God clearly reveals how God dealt with the unbelieving Pharaoh of Egypt (Exodus 7–12). God protected and provided for His people, removed them from Egypt, and the Egyptians perished. Jesus revealed to John the trumpet judgments, which God uses to warn and protect His people during the history of the church, and they are a preview of the more severe vial judgments at the end of time. God has an established pattern of judgments, which include famine, disease, war, and the consequences of man's sinful behaviors. The established judgment pattern of God is what we prayerfully use to interpret the vial judgments.

First Chiasmus

- **Revelation 8:6–7**: " And **the seven angels which had the seven trumpets** prepared themselves to sound. [7] **The first angel sounded, and there followed hail and fire mingled with blood**, and they were cast upon the earth: and the third part of trees was burnt up, and all green grass was burnt up."

- **Revelation 16:1–2**: "And I heard a great voice out of the temple *saying to the seven angels, Go your ways, and pour out the vials of the wrath of God upon the earth.* [2] And *the first went, and poured out his vial upon the earth*; and *there fell a noisome and grievous sore* upon the men which had the mark of the beast, and upon them which worshipped his image."

The trumpet judgments follow the timeline of the seven churches from Revelation 2 and 3. God in His mercy loves all of mankind. God wants all mankind to repent and believe Him.

God sends the trumpet judgments like a mile-marker on the highway telling the traveler how close he is to his final destination. With the proper historical context of each judgment, the Christian can understand how close he is to his final destination of heaven.

The first-century church, represented by Ephesus, obeyed Jesus Christ and spread the gospel. The first angel sounded the trumpet to warn man to repent. John saw hail and fire mingled with blood, which affected one-third of the trees and grass. In prophecy, trees and grass refer to people. Ezekiel describes hail and fire as disease (Ezekiel 38:22).

History records that during the time of the newly established church, the Antonine Plague (AD165–180) decimated the Roman Empire. High fevers, skin sores, diarrhea, and sore throats killed the citizens. An estimated one-third of the residents died during this epidemic. Lost unregenerate man blamed the Christians for their suffering. The unbelievers continued to sacrifice to their unholy gods for healing. In spite of persecution, Christianity continued to grow and spread across the Roman Empire.

At the end of time just before Jesus Christ returns to earth (Revelation 16:1–2), the first angel will pour out the first vial judgment. A noisome and grievous sore will fall upon those who accept the mark of the beast and worship his image. Those who have rejected God's gift of salvation will endure the consequences of their actions. In the last few years since COVID-19, much has been discussed about health. Data now proves that the government-recommended guidelines to curb or prevent the disease were far more detrimental than the disease. Many were deceived, and now many pay the consequence of having bad health.

Before Jesus Christ returns, a *plague* far more intense than man has ever experienced and a man-made *cure* far more detrimental may occur. Gain-of-function research and biological warfare are inventions of man that could cause this plague and decimate the population.

Second Chiasmus

- **Revelation 8:8–9**: "**And the second angel sounded**, and as it were **a great mountain burning with fire was cast into the sea: and the third part of the sea became blood**; 9And the third part of the creatures which were in the sea, and had life, died; and **the third part of the ships were destroyed**."

- **Revelation 16:3**: "And *the second angel poured out his vial* upon the sea; and *it became as the blood of a dead man*: and every living soul died in the sea."

The second angel sounded the trumpet and a third part of the sea became blood. In prophecy, the sea refers to people. The key to understanding this trumpet judgment is the ships. Ships are the economic vitality of a nation. (See 2 Chronicles 9:21, and Ezekiel 27–28.) During the third century, the Roman Empire nearly fell because of its inability to freely trade. The lack of free trade made it harder to keep and maintain large city centers that needed vast amounts of resources. The phrase "give them bread and circuses" was coined so that the citizens would not notice the dire economic conditions. During this time of the Roman Empire, a third of all trade was stopped for various reasons. This period in history correlates with the time of the church at Smyrna. Roman Emperor Diocletian severely persecuted the church for ten years from 303–313. The Roman Empire was reaping the effects of the persecution of God's people.

Prior to the Second Coming of Christ, the second angel pours out his vial upon the sea. The vial judgment like the earlier trumpet judgement affects the economy. The vial judgement is poured out against the beast of globalism. This beast system demands centralized control of all economic activity. The destruction of free trade will eliminate necessary commodities from all continents because of a lack of confidence in credit. Nations plagued with debt can write IOUs for so long before the debt is called. Requiring cash payments for goods will have a cascading effect, which will halt ships at ports or at sea from their final destinations. Tariffs may cause a shortage of goods. The "bread and circus" economy will end, and the sins of a nation must be paid. Economic ruin will affect every nation on earth (Revelation 18:10–11).

Third Chiasmus

- **Revelation 8:10–11**: "And **the third angel sounded**, and there fell a great star from heaven, burning as it were a lamp, and **it fell upon the third part of the rivers, and upon the fountains of waters**; [11] and the name of the star is called Wormwood: . . . because they were made bitter.'"

- **Revelation 16: 4**: "And *the third angel poured out his vial upon the rivers and fountains of waters: and they became blood.*"

The third angel sounded, and a third of the people on earth became bitter and died. The prophet Amos prophesied that those who pervert the justice system cause the wormwood or bitterness (Amos 5:7). The common man thinks he can find no justice because of bribery and fraud in the court system. The "haves" are able to influence the courts while the "have-nots" are given harsh sentences. The hopelessness they feel grows like a cancer. Eventually, the anger bubbles over and the people reject all authority. The people turn to rioting and anarchy.

In the time of the church in Pergamos, Constantine married the church to the state. This unholy union created many hardships for the people. The state forced the people to adopt beliefs they did not want to accept. If citizens of the Roman Empire did not accept the beliefs of the state church, they were excluded from employment, civic functions, and family, or they might even be killed. The coercion by the state and apostate church caused the people to feel great bitterness toward God. This bitterness caused them to harden their hearts and blame God. Anarchy broke out among the people and eventually caused the collapse of the Roman Empire.

The Bible warns that in the last days, perilous times will come. The citizens will be governed by the unlearned, the weak, and the unrighteous. The world's rulers are controlled by their passions of greed and vice. The vilest of men write the laws, control the economies, and oppress the citizens. During the first two vial judgments, the people suffered through plagues of famine and disease caused by the incompetence of their rulers. When the third angel pours out his vial upon the rivers and waters, the people become very bitter. Governments have collapsed because of greed, fraud, injustice, and corruption. Humanity now understands that worldly governments cannot ease their suffering. Their leaders are the problem. The world falls into great despair because man chose to place faith in governments that cannot ease their suffering.

Now comes the anarchy. Humanity rages and seeks vengeance. Cultural wars, race wars, and class wars explode. Everyone blames someone else for their problems. The taste of blood cannot be satisfied. They have made a covenant with death (Isaiah 28:15). The cup of iniquity is very bitter (Revelation 18:5–6).

Fourth Chiasmus

- **Revelation 8:12**: "And **the fourth angel sounded, and the third part of the sun was smitten**, and third part of the moon, and the third part of the stars; so as the third part of them was darkened, and the day shone not for a third part of it, and the night likewise."

- **Revelation 16:8**: "And *the fourth angel poured out his vial upon the sun; and power was given unto him to scorch men with fire.*"

The fourth trumpet judgment occurred during the period of the church in Thyatira. The prophecy was fulfilled during the 1,260-year period of the Dark Ages. The suppression of the Word of God caused the darkness and the time of the Great Tribulation for Christians. Believers were cast from civilization and found safety in caves and mountains. The false church promoted superstitions, paganism, and false teachings. The Word of God was hidden from the people (Revelation 11:3). All biblical knowledge was suppressed to keep the people compliant with the false church's doctrine. The kings and priests prospered and "lived deliciously" while their poor suffered and died from the effects of severe poverty. True believers of God were hunted, tortured, and killed for "the word of their testimony in the blood of the Lamb" (Revelation 12:11). This was indeed a dark, dark period of world history.

The fourth angel pours out the vial upon the sun, and power was given unto him to scorch men with fire. The prophet, Malachi identified Jesus Christ as the Sun of righteousness who will expose all lies (Malachi 4:2). This prophecy will be fulfilled when all the darkness of evil and sin is brought into the light. Glimmers of truth are being exposed today. The lies about COVID-19, of big pharma, big food, and climate change are being brought to light. Podcasts, X, and independent journalists are validating conspiracy theories daily. When the angel pours out this vial, all lies will be exposed. Just as the brightness of the sun purifies, so shall the "Sun of righteousness" offer one last chance of purity to mankind. God uses the 144,000 faithful witnesses of Christ to spread the last message of repentance. God is giving wicked man one last chance the accept His love, grace, and mercy before Jesus Christ returns in the clouds to gather His saints.

Every deception planned in secret by politicians, clergy, kings, rulers, employers, and employees will be revealed. All words spoken in the dark, secret chambers shall be shouted from the housetops (Luke 12:3). No documents or communications will be retracted. The wickedness of secret meetings will be revealed to all.

The first step to repentance is the recognition of sin, the realization that one has broken God's law. Then the sinner makes a choice: Continue in sin, or accept God's grace and free pardon of sin through Jesus Christ. Continuing in sin brings death. Repenting and putting faith in Jesus Christ grants eternal life. God allows man free will to choose his reward: life or death. Will the wicked repent? Or will they blaspheme? Will they blame the 144,000 witnesses for the plagues, for the torment, and for the destruction? Will they demand councils and committees to prove that the witness of Christ is a lie? The world experienced a blame game during the recent COVID-19 plague. It was a pandemic of the "unvaxxed," the unmasked, or those who would not cooperate with the government mandates. That kind of behavior will happen again only worse because the mask of deception has been revealed by the Light of the World, Jesus Christ.

The condemnation or judgment of God is that the Light of the World, Jesus Christ, came into the world, and men loved their evil deeds done in darkness more than the light (John 3:19). Jesus told John the final judgement for unbelievers: "They repented not to give him glory" (Revelation 16:9).

Fifth Chiasmus

- **Revelation 9:1–2, 4–6, 11: "And the fifth angel sounded, and I saw a star fall from heaven unto the earth: and to him was given the key of the bottomless pit. [2] And he opened the bottomless pit; and there arose a smoke out of the pit, as the smoke of a great furnace; and the**

sun and the air were darkened by reason of the smoke of the pit. . . . [4] And **it was commanded them** that they should not **hurt** the grass of the earth, neither any green thing, neither any tree; but **only those men which have not the seal of God in their foreheads.** [5] And to them it was given that **they should not kill them,** but that **they should be tormented five months:** and their torment was as the torment of a scorpion, when he striketh a man. [6] And in **those days shall men seek death, and shall not find it;** and shall desire to die, and death shall flee from them . . . . [11] And **they had a king over them, which is the angel of the bottomless pit,** whose name in the **Hebrew tongue is Abaddon,** but in the **Greek tongue hath his name Apollyon.**"

- **Revelation 16:10–11:** "And *the fifth angel poured out his vial upon the seat of the beast; and his kingdom was full of darkness*; and they gnawed their tongues for pain, [11] *And blasphemed the God of heaven because of their pains and their sores, and repented not of their deeds.*"

The fifth angel sounds the trumpet. John sees a star, which is an angel fall from heaven to earth. When Satan was cast from heaven, God gave him the key to open the bottomless pit. Satan coveted worship in heaven. Now that he has been cast to earth, Satan covets man's worship. The bottomless pit is not a place. It is the deceptions and lies Satan uses to entice men to reject God. Sin's wickedness has no bottom.

The smoke of the great furnace darkened the sun and the air by reason. From the beginning with Adam and Eve, Satan uses reason to cause man to disobey God, "Yea, hath God said" and "Ye shall be as gods, knowing good and evil" (Genesis 3:1, 5). Doubt of the eternal God and the pride of life are the appeals he still uses today. Men try to explain away God with theories of evolution. Man determines what is good or evil, moral or immoral based only on personal satisfaction. Man decides what is for the common good. Becoming a god is amoral. Every man who does what is right in his own eyes is pleasing himself above all others.

Satan denies the truth of God and replaces truth with a lie. "Ye shall not surely die" is the first lie he told to man (Genesis 3:4). God created Adam and Eve and placed them in the perfect environment. God commanded them to not eat of the tree of the knowledge of good and evil because the day they ate, they "shalt surely die" (Genesis 2:17). Satan told Eve the exact opposite of God's command. Since that time, Satan has opposed every commandment of God. As Eve was deceived by his lies, many people today believe Satan's words instead of God's words. The smoke of his lies darkens the light of God's word.

During the fifth trumpet, Satan is allowed to command an army for five months, which is 150 years. This army was not allowed to kill, but they could torment their opponent.

This army was commanded to "hurt only those men which have not the seal of God in their foreheads." The sealed believers of God were protected from any harm. The rise of the Ottoman Empire toward the end of the Dark Ages is the fulfillment of this prophecy.

The Ottoman Empire began attacking the Byzantine Empire on July 27, 1299. One hundred fifty years later, 1449, the Byzantine Emperor was so badly defeated that the Emperor requested permission from the Turks to keep his throne. This fulfilled the five months of torment that John had foretold. During the conquest, the Turks allowed non-Muslim groups to live in their invaded territories. Sealed believers in God lived peacefully in millets, which were religious-based groups. By this arrangement of the Turkish military, the unsealed and the sealed were segregated.[6]

The fifth angel pours out his vial, and the kingdom of Satan is in spiritual darkness. The prophet Elijah preached during the time of King Ahab and his wicked wife, Jezebel (1 Kings 18). Israel had been experiencing a three-and-half year drought, which was causing economic ruin, famine, and disease. King Ahab blamed God's prophet Elijah for the all the trouble in Israel. In the final days, the 144,000 will be blamed for all the troubles of earth. Elijah told the king that it was not his fault for the trouble. King Ahab and Jezebel had led the people away from God. They were forsaking God's commandments and following the false god, Baalim. King Ahab called for a contest to see who was stronger, the prophets of Baal or Elijah.

Jezebel's 450 prophets of Baalim gathered against Elijah, the prophet of God. King Ahab, Queen Jezebel, the priests of Baalim, the citizens of Israel, and Elijah believed he was the only prophet of God remaining. God and one believer are enough to challenge Satan's power. In the final days before Christ comes in the clouds to gather his elect from the earth, the 144,000 will also feel very much alone just as Elijah did. The 144,000 are not a collected group in one part of the world; they are scattered throughout the world preaching the everlasting gospel of Christ.

The prophets of Baal cried all day for their god to answer. They jumped on the altar, screamed, pulled their hair, cut themselves with knives and lancets till the blood gushed out. Their god, Baal, did not answer. The priests became angrier and angrier. Elijah prayed to God asking God to hear him and answer so that all men would know that He is the true God, and all the people need to turn back to Him. Elijah's prayer was answered, and the offering was consumed. The prophets of Baal, the people, King Ahab, and Queen Jezebel did not repent. Instead, in her hatred for Elijah's God, Jezebel wanted to kill Elijah. The darkness of the kingdom of Satan has no light.

In the last days, prophets in the kingdom of darkness continue to worship their false god like the prophets of Baal. Two of the largest religious groups in the world flog themselves, cut themselves, and mark their bodies in worship to their god. The marks of the false kingdom are the same today as in the days of old.

When man blasphemes God and rejects Jesus Christ as the Son of God, man places himself into total spiritual darkness completely separated from the goodness of God. The result of this rejection of the light of God is absolute lawlessness. Anarchy will fill the streets in every city in the world. Satan is the Abaddon, the Apollyon, the one who unlocked the bottomless pit of darkness. Satan reigns in his kingdom of reason on earth.

Sixth Chiasmus

- **Revelation 9:13–15, 21**: "And **the sixth angel sounded**, and I heard a voice from the four horns of the golden altar which is before God, [14] Saying to the sixth angel which had the trumpet, **Loose the four angels which are bound in the great river Euphrates**. [15] And the four angels were loosed, which were **prepared for an hour, and a day, and a month, and a year, for to slay the third part of men. . . .**[21] **Neither repented they** of their murders, nor of their sorceries, nor of their fornications nor of their thefts."

- **Revelation 16:12–16**: "And *the sixth angel poured out his vial upon the great river Euphrates; and the water thereof was dried up*, that the way of the kings of the east might be prepared. [13] And I saw *three unclean spirits*

> *like frogs* come out of the mouth of the *dragon*,
> and out of the mouth of the *beast*, and out of
> the mouth of the *false prophet.* . . . [14] . . . *spir-*
> *its of devils,* . . . . [15] . . . . *Blessed is he that*
> *watcheth, and keepeth his garments*, lest he
> walk naked, and they see his shame. . . . [16] . . .
> *Armageddon.*"

The sixth angel sounds the trumpet, and the four angels, which are bound in the great river Euphrates are loosed. These four demons are prepared for a period of time to slay the third part of men. The Euphrates River fed the Old Testament city of Babylon. Babylon is the name of the apostate church (Revelation 18). Peoples and nations are represented as water. Therefore, the sixth trumpet judgment is describing the battle between two false religious beast systems that history verifies to be the Ottoman Empire and the Roman Catholic Church.

The Ottoman Empire conquered the Byzantine Empire in 1453 with the fall of Constantinople. The Turks continued to battle the Holy Roman Empire to expand their control in Europe. God allowed the beast system of the Ottoman Empire an hour, a day, a month, and a year which is 391 years and 15 days. During this time, the Turks mercilessly invaded Europe, the Middle East, and Northern Africa spreading the religion of Islam. The doctrine they spewed from their mouths promoted a false Christ. This false religious system and the false church from Rome battled each other for religious dominance. They both persecuted God's faithful believers.

The fifth trumpet sound ushered in the first 150 years of the Ottoman Empire. The sixth trumpet sounded to allow the Empire to expand for another 391 years. Jesus revealed to John that the rise of the Ottoman Empire would inflict punishment on the Catholic Church for their persecution of true Christians during the Dark Ages. It also weakened the Catholic Church and eventually led to the Reformation.

On August 11, 1840 the Ottoman Empire sent ambassadors to Europe to elicit help to slow down the invading forces from the Ottoman governor of Egypt. By asking for help from Europe, the Ottoman empire surrendered its sovereignty to foreign nations. It would not be until World War 1 that the Empire finally collapsed. The outreach for help was the first signal of the beginning of the end for the empire. The fifth and sixth trumpet prophecies were fulfilled within the 2,300-year time prophecy revealed to Daniel.

During the same time, the Reformers, Martin Luther and John Calvin, believed this advancement of Islam by the Turks to be the fulfillment of Revelation 9. Luther believed the war to be God's judgment upon the Roman Catholic Church for their sins such as indulgences, papal abuses, idolatry, ritualism, persecution of so-called heretics, and other abuses. "The Turk is the rod of the wrath of the Lord our God and the servant of the raging devil."[7] Luther and Calvin believed that the "fire and brimstone" described by John the Revelator was the Ottoman's use of gunpowder and ammunitions.

Martin Luther believed the "rod of the wrath of the Lord" was a call for his church, the Roman Catholic Church, to repent for its evil deeds. This was not a call to arms or crusades, but a call to repentance before the Holy and Righteous God. Like Elisha, Luther believed God could deliver them (2 Kings 6). The servant of Elisha trembled when he saw the Syrian army coming with horses and chariots to invade Samaria. Elisha prayed that his servant could see that the army of God was much larger and far more powerful. Luther urged his church to believe God was capable of their deliverance.

The sixth angel pours out his vial upon the great river Euphrates, and the waters dry up. This action prepares the way for the kings of the east. Jesus Christ is the King of the East, and it is His return that is being prepared. Isaiah wrote that the righteous man, the Lord, will come from the east (Isaiah 41:2, 4). Jesus told his disciples that at his Second Coming he will come from the east as suddenly and as brightly as lightning (Matthew 24:27).

The Euphrates River, the body of water feeding Babylon, dries up. The Euphrates River represents the people of the world flowing into the false religious systems of Babylon. These apostate religious systems teach another way to God other than Jesus Christ. As Judas Iscariot realized the Priests and Pharisees had lied and deceived him, the world's population will realize that not only have the apostate pagan

systems lied and deceived them, but also the church of Laodicea has deceived them (Jeremiah 16:19). Many who thought
they would escape the wrath of God begin to understand
that they are living through it. They realize they stand lost
and unforgiven before the Righteous God. But instead of
repentance, many take up arms and seek retribution against
the clergy who have fed them lies and deceptions. Judas tried
to give the thirty pieces of silver back to the priests to clear
his conscience (Matthew 27:3–5). The citizens of the world
will lash out in anger at the priests and churches because of
the lies. The time for repentance has passed. The judgment
has been set.

The "four winds of the earth" are now released. As people abandon the houses of false worship, hearts and minds
are turned against all religion. The clergy make one last des-
perate attempt for control. These false prophets of Satan are
being led by the spirits of devils who crave obedience to their
master, Satan, at any cost. The clergy demand the kings and
rulers of governments mandate more restrictive laws to bring
the people back to the church.

When this alliance of Church and State arises to bring
all the world under the rule of the one global church, then
sudden destruction comes from God Almighty in the Battle
of Armageddon. This is the final battle between the demonic
forces of Satan and the force of God. All people on earth will
engage in this battle. Armageddon is not a specific place on
earth. Armageddon is a person's heart and mind that cannot
be changed. The unrepentant mind controlled by demons will

defy all authority and will never bow to the Righteous and Holy God. Unbelievers will experience sudden destruction.

"Multitudes, multitudes in the valley of decision: for the day of the Lord is near in the valley of decision."

—Joel 3:14

Revelation Chapter 4
Throne of God in Heaven

Revelation Chapter 17
Throne of Satan on Earth

What Does This Mean?

In Revelation 4, John describes the throne of God in Heaven. In Revelation 17, John describes the setting of the great whore, the woman sitting on a scarlet-colored beast. This woman is the apostate church and has no authority to enforce her false teachings on the people without the authority of the state. Therefore, the woman sits on the scarlet-colored beast, which is the government that she will use to enforce her doctrine. The historical period for this revelation is from the church at Philadelphia until the present-day church period of Laodicea.

Prior to the Second Coming of Christ, the false church

will again need the state to enforce the worship of the image and the mark of the beast. Jesus Christ reveals these two seats of power to John. The following chiasmus verses are an opposing image of each other. Will man worship God or the apostate church empowered by Satan?

First Chiasmus

- **Revelation 4:2**: "And immediately **I was in the spirit**: and **behold, a throne was set in heaven, and one sat on the throne**."

- **Revelation 17:3**: "So *he carried me away in the spirit into the wilderness*: and *I saw a woman sit upon a scarlet coloured beast*, full of names of blasphemy, having seven heads and ten horns."

John sees a door open in heaven and hears a voice, which sounds like a trumpet talking to him. John has heard this voice before in Revelation 1:10. Jesus Christ invites John to heaven. John is in the spirit in both texts of Revelation 4 and 17. Jesus Christ and the Holy Spirit, the two witnesses of God, are revealing to John details of the "things which must be hereafter" (Revelation 4:1). John is seeing events that no other human being has ever seen. Jesus Christ first reveals to John two different thrones or seats of authority. The first throne is set in heaven. John sees Jesus Christ, the one who sits on the throne of heaven.

In Revelation 17, one of the seven angels with the seven

vials (i.e., judgments) tells John to come and he will show John the judgment of the great whore (v. 1). The angel tells John why the great whore, the false church, is being judged: "With whom the kings of the earth have committed fornication, and the inhabitants of the earth have been made drunk with the wine of her fornication" (Revelation 17:2). This false church has infiltrated the entire earth with her false doctrines, and she has used governments to spread her lies.

The angel carries John into the wilderness (Revelation 17:3). In Scripture, the wilderness is a place of testing, proving, danger, or judgment. The second throne, or seat, John sees in the wilderness is the place of judgment for the great whore. A woman, a church, sits upon a scarlet-colored beast, a kingdom or government. From 1798 till the present, this false church cannot coerce anyone to believe her doctrine because of the laws of separation of church and state. Therefore, she must sit upon a beast, a government, for power. John clearly observes the false church, which throughout the centuries has refused to heed Jesus Christ's plea to repent. John views the history and judgment of the false church.

As stated in the last chapter, when the sixth angel begins to pour out his vial upon the River Euphrates (Revelation 16:12), the people of the earth begin to revolt against the lies of false religion and oppressive governments. The woman as the false religious system believes she can tame the beast, which are the governments headed by the kings of the earth. Both woman and beast believe they are all-powerful and control the universe. The whore and the mighty kings use each other for their selfish benefit.

Both whore and beast deprive humanity of truth. The kings or mighty men of earth realize they have been deceived by the whore and begin to hate her. Humanity's minds are seared with hatred for both. The kings and the people of earth are so drunk on the wine or doctrine of the whore that neither can think clearly. During the vial judgments, few people will seek or find truth.

The world today is reacting like this to governments and religious systems. Many lies have been promoted by both. Some truth is being revealed. The citizens of the world are confused. Many are becoming very angry at the ones who lied and at the ones who are uncovering truth. Man does not know who or what to believe. The public is becoming more frustrated and more distrustful.

Second Chiasmus

- **Revelation 4:3**: "And he that sat was to look upon **like a jasper and a sardine stone**: and there was **a rainbow round about the throne, in sight like unto an emerald**."

- **Revelation 17:4**: And the woman was *arrayed in purple and scarlet colour*, and *decked with gold and precious stones and pearls*, having a golden cup in her hand full of abominations and filthiness of her fornications."

John describes the colors of each throne. The throne of God is like jasper and sardine stone. These stones are red or scarlet representing the shed blood of Jesus Christ. The woman, trying to mimic God, rides a scarlet-colored beast. This is a bloody beast covered in the blood of all the martyred saints.

Next, John sees a rainbow of emerald around the throne. The rainbow is the sign of God's promise to never flood the whole earth again in judgment (Genesis 9:13). The emerald color is a symbol of the resurrection, or new birth, into a new and purer life. Emerald is also the color of truth and love, which perfectly describe the Messiah, Jesus Christ.

The Old Testament prophet, Hosea, uses almost the same words as John to describe this woman (Hosea 2:12–13). She is dressed as a harlot in purple and scarlet; the woman is arrayed with gold and precious stones and pearls. Hosea states these are the rewards from her many lovers. The gold refers to material wealth; precious stones symbolize physical beauty, and pearls are a representation of sexual promiscuity. This woman lusts for admiration from her many lovers.

She promotes the abominations of false doctrines and idolatry. Her filthy fornications mix error with truth. The false church claims to be the way to repentance and salvation instead of the blood of Jesus Christ. God's throne in heaven is one of love and mercy. The whore's throne on earth is one of earthly pleasures and self-admiration.

Third Chiasmus

- **Revelation 4:4**: "And round about the throne were four and twenty seats: and **upon the seats I saw four and twenty elders sitting, clothed in white raiment; and they had on their heads crowns of gold.**"

- **Revelation 17:2**: "*With whom the kings of the earth have committed fornication*, and the inhabitants of the earth have been made drunk with the wine of her fornication."

John sees twenty-four elders clothed in white wearing crowns of gold on their heads and seated around the throne of God. Who are these elders? Much speculation has been made about their identity. John does not identify them. God reveals some facts from His Word about their identity. They are in heaven around the throne of God, so they are no longer living on earth. They were living on earth at one time because they are clothed in white raiment, which "is the righteousness of saints" (Revelation 19:8). A saint is a believer in Jesus Christ who has died. Paul told the Thessalonians that at the Second Coming of Jesus Christ, "the dead in Christ shall rise first" (1 Thessalonians 4:16). How are they seated around the throne of God prior the Second Coming of Christ?

In the Bible, numbers have meaning. The number twenty-four represents the priesthood and worship. The book of Chronicles details the preparations King David of Israel made for the building of the Temple of God. Chronicles 25 describes the separation for service of the musicians for the Temple worship. Twenty-four groups of twelve families were "instructed in the songs of the Lord" to lead the service in worship of God. John sees the twenty-four elders of those families in Revelation 11. Revelation 11:16 says, "And the four and twenty elders, which sat before God on their seats, fell upon their faces, and worshipped God."

In this passage, the twenty-four elders lead the angels in worship of the King of kings prior to His Second Coming to gather His saints. How can redeemed men lead worship in heaven before the Second Coming of Jesus Christ?

Throughout the history of man, God has chosen to take some faithful believers to heaven. God "translated Enoch that he should not see death" (Hebrews 11:5). The prophet "Elijah went up by a whirlwind into heaven" (2 Kings 2:11). Moses died in the land of Moab before going into the Promised Land. No man knew where God buried Moses (Deuteronomy 34:5–6). Jesus Christ contended with the devil about the body of Moses, so Jesus resurrected Moses to heaven (Jude 9). Moses and Elijah appeared with Jesus in their glorified heavenly bodies before Peter, James, and John (Matthew 17:1–3). No man can enter heaven without a changed body like Christ's resurrected body. The twenty-four elders must have glorified bodies like Christ. Therefore, they have been resurrected. When?

Unexplained, extraordinary, heavenly events occurred

during the crucifixion of Jesus Christ. Matthew records what happened when Jesus died:

> Jesus, when he had cried with a loud voice, yielded up the ghost. And behold the veil of the temple was rent in twain from the top to the bottom; and the earth did quake, and the rocks rent; and the graves were opened; and many bodies of the saints which slept arose, and came out of the graves after his resurrection, and went into the holy city, and appeared unto many.
>
> —Matthew 27:50–53

Could it be that these are the twenty-four elders who are now in heaven leading worship?

The Apostle Paul states that Jesus Christ is the "firstfruits of them that slept" (1 Corinthians 15:20). The firstfruits means that Jesus Christ is the surety that all who die in Christ will be raised with an incorruptible, eternal body. Because Jesus Christ lives, we too shall live. Enoch is proof of that promise for those who lived before the flood. Elijah is proof after the flood. Both of those men did not die, but were translated, immediately changed to an eternal body. Moses is the proof of the faithful who do sleep or die and then are resurrected. The opened graves and those who came out after the resurrection of Jesus Christ but before His ascension to heaven are proof that Jesus Christ is the Messiah, the Lamb slain before the foundation of the world, the promised seed, the Son of God, the Savior of man. Therefore, the promise of eternal life is secure in Him. The twenty-four elders may be the ones who received that promise of resurrection, and John saw them worshipping Jesus Christ in heaven. John does not identify them and neither does the Lord. John sees continual worship around the throne of God.

The woman, on the other hand, commits fornication with the kings of the earth. She seduces the kings with her false doctrines much as Satan seduced Eve, "Ye shall be as gods, knowing good and evil" (Genesis 3:4). As long as the whore benefits them, the kings and leaders in government worship and promote her doctrines. Their subjects are made drunk with the wine, doctrine, of her fornication and are unable to discern truth from lies.

Fourth Chiasmus

- **Revelation 4:6a**: "And **before the throne there was a sea of glass like unto crystal:**"

- **Revelation 17:1, 15**: "*I will shew unto thee the judgment of the great whore that sitteth upon many waters*: . . . .* [15] "And he saith unto me, The *waters which thou sawest*, where the whore sitteth, *are peoples, and multitudes, and nations, and tongues.*"

John sees before the throne of God a sea of glass like unto crystal. In Scripture water or sea represents people. John sees

God's people who are dressed in white cleansed by the blood of the Lamb. They are shining brilliantly as a crystal sea before the throne of God.

One of the seven angels with the seven vials tells John to come and see the judgment of the great whore that sits upon many waters. The great whore sits upon her subjects lording over them in absolute tyranny. This marks the beginning of divine judgement of the false religious system that has ruled over many nations.

Jeremiah 51:13 says, "O thou that dwellest upon many waters, abundant in treasures, thine end is come, and the measure of thy covetousness." Quite a contrast! God's people are calm, serene, and secure. The whore's multitudes are agitated like strong waves in the ocean.

Fifth Chiasmus

- **Revelation 4:6b–8**: "And in the midst of the throne, and round about the throne, were **four beasts full of eyes before and behind**. [7] And the **first beast was like a lion**, and **the second beast like a calf**, and **the third beast had a face as a man**, and **the fourth beast was like a flying eagle**. [8] And **the four beasts** had each of them six wings about him; and they were full of eyes within: and **they rest not day and night, saying, Holy, Holy, Holy, Lord God Almighty, which was, and is, and is to come**."

- **Revelation 17:3, 8**: "So he carried me away in the spirit into the wilderness: and I saw a woman sit upon a *scarlet coloured beast, full of names of blasphemy, having seven heads and ten horns.* [8] *. . . the beast that was, and is not, and yet is.*"

John continues to describe the throne of God in heaven. He sees a most unusual sight. Four beasts are in the middle and around the throne. They are full of eyes before and behind. These beasts see everything, everywhere. John is describing the throne of God the best he can with the limited language available to humans. God is omniscient (all-knowing), omnipresent (everywhere), and omnipotent (all-powerful). How can man describe those traits of God adequately? John, a frail man, is confined to space and time. The Old Testament prophets, Isaiah and Ezekiel, were also permitted to view God's throne. Their descriptions complement John's description (Isaiah 6 and Ezekiel 1). God's throne is eternal.

The beasts or creatures represent the holy, eternal kingdom of God. In the book of Numbers Chapter 2, God gave Moses instructions regarding the order of the tribes of Israel as they camped around the Tabernacle during their wilderness journey on the way to the Promised Land. The Apostle Paul wrote that everything the Israelites did on their wilderness journey was for our example (1 Corinthian 10:11). God's ordering of the tribes is a representation of His heavenly kingdom. John observes the beasts around the throne of

God representing the character of the redeemed who make up the Kingdom of Heaven.

The Old and New Testaments proclaim the hope of the kingdom of God. During the time of the Old Testament, God used the nation of Israel to testify of God's law and mercy. The New Testament writers record Jesus establishing his church to equip men with the faith and discipleship needed to enter His presence. John the Baptist preached about the kingdom of heaven. He warned the people to bring forth fruits suitable for repentance (Matthew 3:2; 8). Jesus Christ preached the kingdom of heaven. John sees the hope of God's kingdom fulfilled in heaven.

The first beast John sees is like a lion. "Behold, the Lion of the tribe of Judah," the elders describing Jesus Christ, proclaim to John (Revelation 5:5). In the Israelites' wilderness journey, God instructed the camp of Judah, which included Issachar and Zebulon to pitch on the east side of the Tabernacle. The East gate of the Tabernacle was the entrance for sacrifice and worship. Judah's ensign is the lion. In Israel, their names described their character:

Judah: Now I will praise the Lord.
Issachar: God hath given me my hire.
Zebulon: Now will my husband dwell with me.

The gospel of Matthew in the New Testament presents Jesus Christ as the King of Heaven.

The second beast is like a calf. The camp of Ephraim, composed of Manasseh and Benjamin, is on the west side of the Tabernacle. Ephraim's flag is the bull or ox. Hebrews 9:12 states: "Neither by the blood of goats and calves, but by his own blood he entered in once into the holy place, having obtained eternal redemption for us."

Ephraim: His seed shall become a multitude of nations.
Manasseh: For God hath made me forget all my toil.
Benjamin: Son of the right hand.

The Gospel of Mark presents Jesus Christ as the Servant doing the will of God for man. His blood shed on the cross of Calvary paid the sin debt for all men.

The third beast has a face as a man, which represents Jesus Christ in his humanity as the compassionate Savior. Jesus as a man faced the temptations of the flesh, yet He lived a sinless life on earth. Hebrews 4:15 declares: "For we have not an high priest which cannot be touched with the feeling of our infirmities; but was in all points tempted like as we are, yet without sin."

The camp of Reuben along with Simeon and Gad camped on the south of the Tabernacle:

Reuben: Surely the Lord hath looked upon mine affliction.
Simeon: The Lord hath heard I was hated.
Gad: A troop cometh.

The Gospel of Luke presents Jesus Christ as the Son of Man showing love and compassion to man. He healed the sick; made the lame to walk, the blind to see, the deaf to hear; cast out demons; and fed the hungry. Jesus healed the broken spirits of all who called on His name. No one was denied God's free pardon of sin.

The fourth beast is like a flying eagle. An eagle represents strength, freedom, victory, and majesty. The camp of Dan with Naphtali and Asher camped on the north side of the Tabernacle. The tribe of Dan was represented by the eagle.

> Dan: Shall judge his people; I have waited for thy salvation.
> Naphtali: I have prevailed (overcome).
> Asher: Will call me blessed.

The Gospel of John presents Jesus Christ as God, King of kings. Jesus Christ gained the victory over sin, death, and the grave:

- **Isaiah 25:8**: "He will swallow up death in victory."

- **1 Corinthians 15:55**: "O death, where is thy sting? O grave, where is thy victory?"

God instructed the priestly tribe of Levi to be responsible for all phases of worship in the Tabernacle. Jesus Christ is the believer's great High Priest who mediates between man and God in the Temple in Heaven. God's Holy Tabernacle was the Israelites' center of life. Jesus Christ is the center of life in the Kingdom of Heaven. As Savior and Lord, Jesus Christ should occupy the center of each believer's heart.

In the Kingdom of Heaven, the four beasts around the throne continually worship Jesus Christ, the Lord God Almighty **which was** in the beginning with God; **which is** as a man on earth living a sinless life; **which is to come** at His Second Coming in the clouds of heaven. The presence of the four beasts verifies that all believers are joint heirs with Christ in His heavenly kingdom and will continually worship God around His throne.

The scarlet-colored beast John describes in Revelation 17 is very different from the beasts worshipping around the throne of God. The red beast is a kingdom full of blasphemy and anger. Blasphemy is doing evil or speaking evil about God. The red beast kingdom wants worship and totally rejects Jesus Christ.

The king of the scarlet beast kingdom gives power to the false church, the woman. The king of this violent, blasphemous kingdom ascends out of the bottomless pit. Satan is clearly identified as the king of the bottomless pit in Revelation 9:1, which says, "I saw a star [angel] fall from heaven unto the earth: and to him was given the key of the bottomless pit."

Abaddon and Apollyon mean "A Destroyer." Satan is given the key or the authority from God to prove or test those who dwell on the earth. God always gives man freedom of choice. Satan is given this authority for a short time.

The **beast that was** began during the days of Constantine. The **beast that is not** was removed in 1798 at the end of the French Revolution. The **beast that yet is** began to regain power over the world again in 1929.

Unbelievers on earth will "wonder" when they behold this beastly kingdom. They will become bewitched or fascinated by the false representation of the gospel of Christ. Those who are deceived and believe the lies of the false church will reject Jesus Christ as their personal Savior. Their names will not be recorded in the Lamb's Book of Life. Unbelievers, Satan, the beast, and the false church will go into perdition, which is utter destruction.

> Let no man deceive you . . . that man of sin be revealed, the son of perdition; [4] Who opposeth and exalteth himself above all that is called God. . . . [8] And then shall that Wicked be revealed, whom the Lord shall consume . . . and shall destroy with the brightness of his coming. . . . [11]And . . . God shall send them strong delusion, that they should believe a lie: [12] that they all might be damned who believed not the truth, but had pleasure in unrighteousness.
>
> —2 Thessalonians 2:3–4, 8, 11–12

During this time of the end of man's history on earth, no one is able to oppose the scarlet beast system controlled by Satan. This government is the image of the first beast of Revelation 13. The false church is a tool of this wicked government to further the power of Satan. That Wicked one, Satan, covets the worship of all men, and he will get it by force.

Sixth Chiasmus

- **Revelation 4:5**: "And out of the throne proceeded lightnings and thunderings and voices: and there were **seven lamps of fire burning before the throne**, which are the seven Spirits of God."

- **Revelation 17:5**: "And upon her forehead was a name written, *Mystery, Babylon the Great, the Mother of Harlots and Abominations of the Earth*."

John sees proceeding from the throne of God lightning, and he hears thunder and voices. Lightning and thunder are indicative of righteous judgment. When God gave His Law to the people of Israel from Mount Sinai, Moses experienced the same power of God as John.

> And it came to pass on the third day in the morning, that there were thunders and lightnings, and a thick cloud upon the mount, and the voice of the trumpet exceeding loud; so that all the people that was in the camp trembled.
>
> —Exodus 19:16

John observed the Lord's churches as seven lamps of fire burning before the throne (Revelation 1:20). God's churches have his undivided attention. The Holy Spirit kindles a flame in each member to live a message of love, joy, peace, long suffering, gentleness, goodness, faith, meekness, and temperance in a sin-filled world. The small lamp of each believer shines as the sun in a world filled with darkness from sin.

The woman, the mother of the harlot churches, promotes a religious movement of mystery and abominations. She works though secret societies and organizations. She is drunken with the blood of the saints and martyrs of Jesus Christ. For nearly 2,000 years, this false religious system has tried to extinguish the light of the gospel by persecuting those proclaiming it or by perverting the simple message of Jesus Christ as Savior of the world.

The woman is the Roman Catholic church and her daughters are all the Protestant churches who have signed ecumenical documents professing the doctrines of the mother. These churches are now the harlots who promote her abominations. Idolatry, lies, arrogant conceit, abortion, deceit, riots, finding fault in others, sexual perversions, willful disobedience to all authority, social unrest are just a few of the cultural and social reforms promoted by the false churches (Proverbs 6:16–19). Religious organizations promoting social justice over God's justice will bring the wrath of God.

Today, the true church of God must burn as lamps shining forth the light of the glorious gospel to this dark world.

Seventh Chiasmus

- **Revelation 4:10–11**: "**The four and twenty elders fall down before him that sat on the throne, and worship him that liveth for ever and ever, and cast their crowns** before the throne, saying, [11] Thou art worthy, O Lord, to receive glory and honour and power: **for thou hast created all things, and for thy pleasure they are and were created.**"

- **Revelation 17:16–17**: "*And the ten horns which thou sawest upon the beast, these shall hate the whore*, and shall make her desolate and naked, and shall eat her flesh, and burn her with fire. [17] *For God hath put in their hearts to fulfil his will, and to agree, and give their kingdom unto the beast, until the words of God shall be fulfilled.*"

John sees the kingdom of heaven as one of joy, harmony and unity. The twenty-four elders were resurrected with Jesus Christ; they represent all the redeemed of Christ. At Christ's coming, all believers will receive a crown of glory (1 Peter 5:4), a crown of righteousness (2 Timothy 4:8), and a crown of rejoicing (1 Thessalonians 2:19). Every believer who overcomes temptations will receive an incorruptible crown of life (James 1:12; 1 Corinthians 9:25). Soon all the redeemed will join the twenty-four elders in worship to their eternal God, the Creator of all things. The saints of God will sing praises forever and cast their crowns before His throne.

John states that the ten horns upon the beast hate the whore and want to destroy her. The ten horns were the original provinces of the Western Roman Empire. These European countries colonized the rest of the world and spread the religion of the apostate church. The beast is the United States of America combined with all the globalist organizations of the world such as the WHO, WEF, UN, EU, and NATO. All these organizations want to create a new world order. The ten horn nations "give their kingdom" to the authority of the beast of the United States. These nations hate the whore and want her destroyed. Why?

In the future, the second beast of Revelation 13, the United States of America, will make an image to the first beast, the Roman Catholic Church. Everyone on earth will be required to take the mark of the first beast to buy or sell and will be required to worship the first beast. Will this be the reason for the ten nations' hatred?

The Roman Catholic Church began in Rome, and she consumed the kingdoms of Europe throughout the Middle Ages. Could European nations become jealous or fearful of the church's union with the powerful United States? Do nations fear a loss of authority? Do the nations become fearful that the church will take their place of authority? Are the nations afraid of being consumed again? Have nations grown tired of being manipulated by her?

In the last days before the return of Christ, these countries and organizations will turn against the apostate church. Their anger will be so great that nations worldwide will condemn all religion. When all religion is removed, the new world order globalist system will gain total control of the world's population. This is their agenda. God has put in their hearts to fulfil his will, and the words of God shall be fulfilled. Christians should not be overly concerned about the future events. We have the promises of Psalm 91, and all of God's words shall be fulfilled.

When the kings of the earth turn against the Roman Catholic Church and remove her authority, then great economic destruction will fall on the world; this will fulfill God's judgment on Babylon.

> Standing afar off for the fear of her torment, saying, Alas, alas, that great city Babylon, that mighty city! For in one hour is thy judgment come, [11]And the merchants of the earth shall weep and mourn over her; for no man buyeth their merchandise any more."
>
> —Revelation 18:10–11

Total economic ruin consumes the world. Mankind is consumed by the evilness of his works. Great sin has great consequences causing all humanity to suffer. Now "the four winds of the earth" (Revelation 7:1) are unleashed. War consumes the planet.

Revelation Chapters 5
Worthy is the Lamb

Revelation Chapter 18
Babylon is Fallen

What Does This Mean?

John is permitted to observe a most important scene in heaven. God has a book sealed with seven seals. A strong angel inquires who is worthy to open the book. A search was made in heaven and earth for the one worthy to open the sealed book of the redeemed. No one was found. John weeps as one without hope. If no one is found worthy to open the book, all is lost. No man will enter heaven and enjoy the presence of God. One of the elders assures John that the Lion of the tribe of Judah, the Root of David, is worthy. A Lamb, looking as it had been slain, Jesus Christ, stands from the midst of the throne and takes the book from the hand of

God. The four beasts, the twenty-four elders, and billions of angels sing and worship the Lamb who lives for ever and ever. God's promises are sure.

Revelation 18 details the Lamb's judgment of Babylon, the antichrist false religious/political system of the world. God's people are cautioned to come out of that false system so they will not receive her plagues. False religion, kings of the earth, the rich merchants, the entertainers, and all who lived life selfishly while taking advantage of other people's misfortunes will be judged according to their works. The worldly antichrist system will be rewarded double unto double for its iniquities and mistreating believers of God. God's promises are sure.

These Chiasmus verses contrast the scene in heaven with the scene on earth.

First Chiasmus

- **Revelation 5:1–2**: "And I saw in the right hand of him that sat on the throne **a book written within and on the backside**, sealed with seven seals. [2] And **I saw a strong angel proclaiming with a loud voice**, Who is worthy to open the book, and to loose the seals thereof?

- **Revelation 18:1–2**: "And after these things *I saw another angel* come down from heaven, having great power; and the earth was lightened with his glory. [2] And *he cried mightily with a strong* *voice*, . . . [4] ***Come out of her, my people***, that ye be not partakers of her sins, and that ye receive not of her plagues.

John is permitted to see God sitting on his throne holding a sealed book in his right hand. A strong angel proclaims loudly, "Who is worthy to open the book, and to loose the seals thereof" (Revelation 5:2)? Someone equal to God is the only one worthy to have the authority to open the seals. What is in this sealed book that is so important? The prophets Ezekiel, Isaiah, and Zechariah were given sealed books or a book written on both sides from God. Their books hold a clue to the contents of this book in heaven.

Ezekiel was given a book written on both sides (Ezekiel 2–3). His book was one of great sorrow, grief, or distress. Ezekiel was told to eat the book. It would be sweet as honey in his mouth, but would make his belly bitter. Ezekiel's message to the unrighteous was to turn from their sinful ways and obey God. Ezekiel is warning the righteous to remain faithful. Jesus warned his disciples that trouble would come throughout the history of the church (Matthew 24). Wars, famine, disease, and persecutions will afflict all people on earth. This will be a time of bitterness. The faithful are to keep their faith, obey God, and warn others to believe in Him also.

Isaiah was given a sealed book for the learned or unlearned (Isaiah 29:11–15). The learned are those who are able to understand the language of the book (Ezekiel 3:6).

The unlearned are those who are unable to understand the language of the book. The book of Jonah is an example of taking the gospel to the unlearned. God instructed Jonah to go to a foreign nation, Nineveh, who had never heard the Word of God. God wanted Jonah to warn the people to repent because judgment was coming. Even though the people of Nineveh spoke a different language, they harkened to the voice of Jonah. God's message is for all who will listen. The gospel of Christ is not hidden to those who seek it.

Isaiah's message in his book was for those who claim to be righteous. They speak words that honor God. They claim to be followers of Christ. They do marvelous works of charity that are honored by men. Yet, their hearts are far from God.

The learned men during the time of Jesus Christ constantly found fault with Him and his disciples because they did not follow the traditions of the elders (Mark 7:5–9). Jesus called the Pharisees and scribes hypocrites because they honored Him with their mouths and actions, but their hearts were far from God. They worshipped God in vain and taught their traditions as doctrines. They taught "Corban" as a work of charity and honor, but Jesus knew they had neglected the fifth commandment of honoring mother and father for their traditions of charity. Churches today neglect the commandments of God by teaching the traditions of men.

Zechariah looked and beheld a flying roll (Zechariah 5:1,

3–4). Those who blaspheme the name of God teaching salvation by another way other than the blood of Jesus Christ steal men's souls. The blasphemer and the one believing the false message are both cut off.

The message from the three prophets is for the church of Laodicea (Revelation 3:14–22). The church of today believes they are rich and in need of nothing. God tells them they are poor, wretched, miserable, blind, and naked. Jesus promises that where two or three are gathered together in His name, He is with them (Matthew 18:20). Jesus Christ is outside the church at Laodicea knocking on the door wanting to come inside. The church no longer recognizes sin. The church has forsaken the law of God and has accepted the traditions of men.

Ezekiel warned the righteous to be a watchman over the house of God. Stay true to the Word of God. The church is to warn the unrighteous to repent and obey God and to follow the commandments of God, not the traditions of man. Zechariah warned that those who profess the name of God but teach a false gospel are blasphemers. The church and those who believe her false message will be cut off.

The message of the book that Jesus Christ is worthy to open is proclaimed throughout the Word of God to everyone. The sealed book is the book of redemption of Christ. Revelation 14:12 says, "Here is the patience of the saints: here are they that keep the commandments of God, and the faith of Jesus."

In Revelation 18 John sees another angel coming down

from heaven to earth. This angel cries mightily with a strong voice warning the inhabitants of earth that Babylon is fallen. Satan brought his war against Christ in heaven to earth into the false Babylonian system of worship. Babylon is not a place, but a mindset controlled by devils and evil spirits. Babylon is the false antichrist system that replaces Jesus Christ with the precepts and traditions of men. Another gospel is preached instead of faith in Jesus Christ and obeying his commandments. Any church or organization replacing the blood of Christ for the redemption of man's sins with any other method of salvation is in Babylon. Babylon teaches a message of tolerance and does not recognize sin. Babylon will not stand under the judgment of Jesus Christ. The angel pleads, "Come out of her, my people, that ye be not partakers of her sins, and that ye receive not of her plagues" (Revelation 18:4).

Second Chiasmus

- **Revelation 5:4**: "**And I wept much**, because no man was found worthy to open and to read the book, neither to look thereon."

- **Revelation 18:9**: "And *the kings of the earth*, who have committed fornication and lived deliciously with her, *shall bewail her, and lament for her*, when they shall see the smoke of her burning."

- **Revelation 18:11**: "And *the merchants of the earth shall weep and mourn over her*; for no man buyeth their merchandise any more."

John observes that no man in heaven or in earth is able or worthy to open and to read, neither to look upon this book. This causes John to weep in utter despair as a man with no hope.

John observes the kings and merchants on earth also weeping and mourning but for different reasons. They lament the loss of power and riches because of their association with the false religious/political system on earth. This system has enriched them mightily, so when she falls, they weep over the loss of personal gain.

John is experiencing a spiritual loss while the kings and merchants on earth are experiencing a worldly physical loss. These are two completely different mindsets or perceptions of the problem. John is fearing an eternal loss; whereas, the kings and merchants are fearing an immediate loss.

Third Chiasmus

- **Revelation 5:6**: "**Stood a Lamb as it had been slain,** having seven horns and seven eyes, which are the seven Spirits of God sent forth into all the earth."

- **Revelation 18:7**: "*I sit a queen, and am no widow, and shall see no sorrow.*"

John sees the Lamb of God, Jesus Christ, standing in the midst of the throne, surrounded by the four beasts and the elders. "A Lamb as it had been slain" is the perfect description of Jesus Christ. In the tabernacle system of worship, a lamb of the first year was required as a sacrifice. A cuddly lamb pure, innocent, and playful must be killed for the sins of an individual. What kind of person would want to continue to sin knowing a baby lamb would pay the price? Sin is ugly. It is evil and causes bad consequences for the sinner and those around him. Our Heavenly Father and Christ hate sin because it hurts all creation.

John has experienced great emotions. He wept uncontrollably with great sorrow when he believed that eternal life would not be available because no one was found to open the book. Now that one is found, it is a beaten and bloody Lamb savagely slain for the sins of man. John feels guilt and shame for himself and all sinners who murdered the Lamb. One day all who have been redeemed by the blood of the Lamb will see the marks of his savage slaying for sins. May we see that vision now and live obedient lives that are worthy of his sacrifice.

In contrast, John sees a queen who has no shame, sorrow, or guilt. She does not see her sin. The mother of harlots sits as a queen and glorifies herself in all she does demanding complete obedience from her subjects. False churches, big business, and governments are in union with the woman. She sacrifices nothing and has no remorse taking from those who support her lavish life style. She is a lost and destitute church teaching the traditions of men as doctrines of God. The blood of saints fills her cup of iniquity. This church commits blasphemy believing she sits in the seat of God blessing her followers. God will reward all who have taken advantage of others double according to her works. The arrogance of this woman knows no bounds.

Revelation Chapter 6

The Seals and the Four Horsemen

Revelation Chapters 19 and 20

The White Horse Rider

What Does This Mean?

In these chapters Jesus Christ will begin to open the seals of the book. John will observe the history of God's people in a battle with Satan and his army until the return of Jesus Christ.

The four horsemen in Revelation 6 have been the source of much speculation. God gave Zechariah a vision of these same horsemen (Zechariah 6:1–8). Zechariah saw four chariots come out from between two mountains of brass. God often interacted with man from a mountain such as Mount Sinai, Mount Carmel, and Mount Horeb. Brass symbolizes judgment or strength. The four horses represent the four spirits of heaven coming from God's place of judgment. The four spirits are mindsets of beliefs or convictions. Man is created with a free will. He can choose to believe the Spirit of God or man can choose to believe the spirits of devils.

Zechariah saw four chariots each one pulled by a different color horse. The horses were red, black, white, and speckled pale gray. The red and speckled pale gray horses go toward the south and "walk to and fro through the earth." Who else walks to and fro through the earth? Satan. He boasted to God that he walks to and fro and up and down in the earth (Job 1:7). Therefore, the red and speckled pale gray horses represent spirits of devils who tempt men, take away peace, and steal men's souls. The black and white horses represent the Spirit of God that goes toward the north country, and they bring peace, contentment, and soothe men's souls.

First Chiasmus

- **Revelation 6:2**: "And I saw, and **behold a white horse**: and he that sat on him had a bow; and **a crown was given unto him**: and **he went forth conquering, and to conquer**."

- **Revelation 19:11–12, 16**: "And I saw heaven opened, and *__behold a white horse__*; and he that sat upon him was called Faithful and True, and in righteousness *__he doth judge and make war__*. [12]

His eyes were as a flame of fire, and **on his head were many crowns**; and he had a name written, that no man knew, but he himself. [16] And he hath on his vesture and on his thigh a name written, King of Kings, and Lord of Lords."

John sees a rider on a white horse whose name is King of Kings, and Lord of Lords. Jesus Christ is the King who wears many crowns; He judges and makes war, and He is the one who conquers. John is seeing the gospel cover the entire world. The first-century church represented by Ephesus (Revelation 2:1–7) carried the gospel throughout the known world. They rejected false teachings and reproved men of their sins. They also hated the deeds of the Nicolaitans, which is pastor rule. They were the true watchmen for the cause of Christ.

Second Chiasmus

- **Revelation 6:4**: "And there went out another horse that was red: and power was given to him that sat thereon **to take peace from the earth, and that they should kill one another**: and there was given unto him a great sword."

- **Revelation 19:19**: "And I saw the beast, and the kings of the earth, and their armies, gathered together *to make war against him that sat on the horse*, and against his army.

Jesus Christ opens the second seal. John sees a red horse. Power is given to the rider of the red horse to take peace from the earth, which causes death. Zechariah identified the red horse rider as the one who goes "to and fro" in the earth. Job identifies the one going to and fro in the earth as Satan. Power was given to the rider of this horse. God is the only One who can give power. Satan must receive power, or permission, from God to act as seen in the example of Job (Job 1:11). The mindset of Satan is war and destruction of Jesus Christ and His followers. Jesus warned His disciples of wars and rumors of war. In Matthew 24:7, Jesus says, "For nation shall rise against nation, and kingdom against kingdom."

Satan gathers the beast, the false religious system and the kings of the nations with their armies to make war against the rider of the white horse and his army which is Jesus Christ and his faithful followers.

Jesus described what Paul and other missionaries throughout history have encountered. Paul carried the gospel to Galatia. False prophets, sorcerers, demonic spirits, and unbelievers tried to stop Paul from preaching to hinder others from believing the gospel. Some unbelievers stoned Paul leaving him for dead. Their resistance to the gospel message caused the new converts of Galatia to doubt their new found peace with God through belief in Jesus Christ. Paul was surprised that they were so quickly departed from the faith of Christ. He wondered who had deceived them into believing another gospel (Galatians 1:6–8, 3:1).

In the church in Smyrna, peace was taken away from

the newly converted believers by severe persecutions (Revelation 2:8–11). For ten years, the Roman Emperor Diocletian hunted and killed the Christians trying to stop the gospel of Christ. Those who follow the red horse rider hinder the gospel of Christ. They are unbelieving deceivers who have the mindset of Satan.

Third Chiasmus

- **Revelation 6:5–6**: "And when he had opened the third seal, I heard the third beast say, Come and see. And I beheld, and lo **a black horse**; and **he that sat on him had a pair of balances in his hand**. ⁶ And I heard a voice in the midst of the four beasts say, A measure of wheat for a penny, and three measures of barley for a penny; and **see thou hurt not the oil and the wine**."

- **Revelation 19:2, 9**: "*For true and righteous are his judgments*: for he hath judged the great whore, which did corrupt the earth with her fornication, and hath avenged the blood of his servants at her hand. ⁹And he saith unto me, Write, Blessed are they which are called unto the *marriage supper of the Lamb*. And he saith unto me, These are the true sayings of God."

Jesus Christ opens the third seal. John sees a rider on a black horse with balances in his hand. The prophet Zechariah saw the black horses go into the north country with the white horses. These horses quiet the spirit in the north country. Paul wrote "to be spiritually minded is life and peace" (Romans 8:6). The rider of the black horse brings life and peace.

The rider of this horse is the one who holds the balances in his hand. A pair of balances is a standard of measurement. The rider of the black horse determines or judges the value of one thing compared to another. Jesus Christ is the one who brings eternal life and peace with God. Jesus Christ is the True and Righteous Judge. Therefore, Jesus Christ is the rider of the black horse.

John hears a voice telling the measures and worth of wheat and barley. Wheat and barley are used to make bread. A measure of wheat and three measures of barley are enough to make about one gallon of flour or four loaves of bread. The amount of manna allotted for each person during the Exodus from Egypt was an Omer or about two quarts. Jesus Christ is the bread of life, the manna from heaven. "See thou hurt not the oil and the wine," says the voice from the Throne of heaven. The oil represents the Holy Spirit. The wine represents the blood of Jesus Christ.

The truth of the Word of God is the gospel of Christ. Jesus holds the balances measuring our character. A Christian's character should reflect the bread of life, our Lord and Savior. Believers should be filled with the oil of the Spirit and be full of the wine of the Word of God. In these last days Christians do not want to be found wanting or running short of truth from the Word of God.

As persecution of Jesus Christ's church increases during these last days, believers will need more of the attitude of Christ to overcome till the Second Coming. This may explain the double portion of bread. Christians will value their faith, the Word, and their obedience to God as worthy unto death (Revelation 12:11). The unbelieving world will view faith, the Word, and Jesus Christ as meaningless—worth mere pennies.

The church at Pergamos was given to eat the hidden manna, the Word of God. They were also told to hold fast and true to the name of Jesus Christ in the face of persecutions (Revelation 2:12–17). The believers of God are sealed with the steadfast hope of their salvation. In the present day, believers in churches observe the Lord's Supper remembering the Savior's suffering and shame for payment of mankind's sins. The overcomer's hope is to one day hear the words of our Blessed Savior: "Blessed are they which are called unto the marriage supper of the Lamb. And he saith unto me, These are the true sayings of God (Revelation 19:9)."

Fourth Chiasmus

- **Revelation 6:8**: "And I looked, and behold a pale horse: and his name that sat on him was Death, and Hell followed with him. And power was given unto them over the fourth part of the earth, **to kill with sword, and with hunger, and with death, and with the beast of the earth.**"

- **Revelation 18:8, 11**: "*Therefore shall her plagues come in one day, death, and mourning, and famine;* and she shall be utterly burned with fire: for strong is the Lord God who judgeth her. [11] *And the merchants of the earth shall weep and mourn over her;* for no man buyeth their merchandise any more."

Jesus removes the fourth seal, and a terrible scene unfolds. The pale horse rider is Death, and Hell followed him. Power was given the rider of the pale horse to kill a fourth part of the earth with the sword, with hunger, and with torture. The beast false religious system of the earth aided the rider Death in his pursuit of destruction. Satan is clearly the rider of Death, the pale horse. Zechariah confirms his identity. The speckled pale gray horses go forth toward the south country walking to and fro seeking whom they may devour.

Christianity was overtaking the world, and Satan had to stop it. During the church period of Thyatira, Satan married the Roman Church to the Roman Empire creating the Holy Roman Empire (Revelation 2:18–29). Satan used this unholy union to persecute millions of Christians. The false church/state system, Jezebel, burned Christians at the stake, destroyed Bibles, and made war with God's people during the 1,260 years of Great Tribulation during the Dark Ages. The faithful sealed of God kept the words of God. The pure gospel entered the great tribulation, and 1,260 years later, the pure gospel of Jesus Christ emerged from the darkness.

Today Christians are again the most persecuted people on earth. The mindset of Satan and his followers is death and destruction. The attitude of death is clearly evident in the culture of abortion, the religion of climate change, atheism, communism, cultural Christianity, and in all who desire complete control over the lives of other humans. The unholy beast system of false religion will one day be judged severely. Death, mourning, and famine will be her reward for her wicked works against God's faithful. As she has treated the Christians, so shall the unholy, wicked men of the earth treat her.

Fifth Chiasmus

- **Revelation 6:9–11**: "And when he had opened the fifth seal, **I saw under the altar the souls of them that were slain for the word of God, and for the testimony which they held**: [10] And they cried with a loud voice, saying, **How long, O Lord, holy and true, dost thou not judge and avenge our blood on them that dwell on the earth**? [11] And white robes were given unto every one of them; and **it was said unto them, that they should rest yet for a little season, until their fellowservants also and their brethren, that should be killed as they were, should be fulfilled**."

- **Revelation 20:4**: "And I saw thrones, and they sat upon them, and judgment was given unto them: and *I saw the souls of them that were beheaded for the witness of Jesus, and for the word of God, and which had not worshipped the beast, neither his image, neither had received his mark upon their foreheads, or in their hands*; and they lived and reigned with Christ a thousand years."

Jesus opens the fifth seal. John sees the martyrs of God from all generations. God is aware of every soul who has lost their life for the Word of God and the testimony of Jesus Christ. Just as Abel's blood cried from the ground after Cain killed him (Genesis 4:10), the blood of every persecuted slain saint of God cries from the ground for vengeance and judgment. God hears them and comforts them telling them to continue in their sleep in the grave until all the saints of God have died for their faith. God's children have not been removed from danger in the past, or now in the present, and will not be removed from danger in the future. Christians are persecuted and killed daily. After Satan's mob has slain the last Christian, God's mighty hand of judgment will avenge all his children in absolute righteousness. Vengeance and judgment belong to the Lord. Obedience to His Word belongs to the overcomer in Christ.

Jesus told the church at Sardis to continue to watch and stengthen the doctrines (Reveleation 3:1–6). Continue preaching and teaching the gospel of Christ. Continue warning men to repent and obey the Lord.

Sixth Chiasmus

The Signs of the End Times

Humans have a natural curiosity about the future. God's Word records two groups of people who asked Jesus to tell them about future events. The Pharisees and Sadducees did not believe Jesus Christ was the Messiah, the Son of God (Matthew 16:1–4). They had observed his teaching and miracles, but still denied that He was the Savior. Their motive was to tempt, mock, deny, and ridicule him. Their desire for a sign from heaven was not to prepare themselves for the kingdom of heaven, but to know how long they could please their fleshly desires on earth. Jesus told them signs of the weather. Jesus also gave them the sign of the prophet Jonah, which is a picture of Jesus's death, burial, and resurrection. They needed to believe Jesus was their Savior before they could prepare for the kingdom of heaven.

Jesus Christ's disciples were the other group to ask about signs of the end of the world. Their desire was to prepare themselves for the kingdom of heaven. Matthew 24 is the answer to their questions. The events Jesus described to his disciples are the same events John sees when Jesus opens the sixth seal. The verses of Matthew 24 complement the sixth seal of Revelation 6.

- **Revelation 6:12–14**: "And I beheld when **he had opened the sixth seal**, and, lo, **there was a great earthquake**; and **the sun became black as sackcloth of hair**, and **the moon became as blood**; [13] And **the stars of heaven fell unto the earth**, even as a fig tree casteth her untimely figs, when she is shaken of a mighty wind. [14] And **the heaven departed as a scroll**, when it is rolled together; and **every mountain and island were moved out of their places**."

- **Matthew 24:29–30**: "Immediately after the tribulation of those days *shall the sun be darkened, and the moon shall not give her light, and the stars shall fall from heaven*, and the powers of the heavens shall be shaken: [30] And *then shall appear the sign of the Son of man in heaven*: and then shall all the tribes of the earth mourn, and *they shall see the Son of man coming in the clouds of heaven with power and great glory*."

At the opening of the sixth seal, John beholds a series of events signaling the end of time on earth. At the closing of the Dark Ages, history records several of these events as having occurred in the order John sees them happen. The first event he saw was a great earthquake. The great Lisbon earthquake of 1755 was felt among most of the known world.[8] In 1780, the great dark day happened in New England with the moon looking like blood that night.[9] The great meteor shower of 1833 was explained as if all the stars were coming from one central location and falling to the earth.[10]

The church in Philadelphia was the period that experienced these signs of the times. During this time in history, Bible institutes and colleges were expanding around the world. Missionaries were taking the gospel to places that had never heard the Word of God preached. Satan's forces were busy pushing communism, evolution, textual criticism, and humanism. Jesus commended this church for keeping the Word pure.

The next major event to occur is heaven departing as a scroll. This will happen at the Second Coming of Jesus Christ. In **Matthew 24:36**, Jesus says, "But of that day and hour knoweth no man, no, not the angels of heaven, but my Father only."

The blood of Jesus Christ seals the elect of God. Because of their faith in Jesus Christ, they are looking for His coming. The Pharisees, the Sadducees, and other nonbelievers in Jesus Christ will experience the great day of God's wrath. Now is the day to choose Christ.

Seventh Chiasmus

- **Revelation 6:15–17: "And the kings of the earth, and the great men, and the rich men, and the chief captains, and the mighty men, and every bondman, and every free man, hid themselves in the dens and in the rocks of the** mountains; ¹⁶ **And said to the mountains and rocks, Fall on us, and hide us from the face of him that sitteth on the throne, and from the wrath of the Lamb:** ¹⁷ **For the great day of his wrath is come; and who shall be able to stand?"**

- **Revelation 20:11–12**: "And I saw a great white throne, and him that sat on it, from whose face the earth and the heaven fled away; and there was found no place for them. *¹²And I saw the dead, small and great, stand before God; and the books were opened: and another book was opened, which is the book of life: and the dead were judged out of those things which were written in the books, according to their works.*"

Revelation 6:14–17 is a continuation of the opening of the sixth seal. Today, the whole world sees the signs of His coming. Project 2025, Agenda 2030, prayer apps, religious movies, and podcasts are devoted to the Second Coming of Christ and the end of the world. Rich men are building bunkers in the mountains for safety. Spaceships are being built to inhabit Mars when Earth is no longer habitable.

The Pharisees and Sadducees saw the miracles, teachings, crucifixion, resurrection, and ascension of Jesus Christ, yet they continued to reject Him. They refused to repent and humble themselves to God. The unbelieving people on earth today are doing the same as the Pharisees. Unbelieving humanity would rather hide their face from God than to obey His Word and repent. These are those who love their life unto death and will be judged according to their works. "He that loveth his life shall lose it" (John 12:25).

The church of Laodicea is the church who will see the return of Christ. The kings of the earth, great men, rich men, chief captains, mighty men, bondmen, and free men live during this historical period. This church does not believe they have a need for Christ. They are neither hot or cold, but satisfied with life on earth. They have no vision of heavenly things. Jesus urges the faithful remnant to continue to watch, be zealous, rebuke sin, and preach repentance because He is coming soon.

The Return of Jesus Christ

"And when he had opened **the seventh seal**, there was silence in heaven about the space of half an hour" (Revelation 8:1).

Jesus Christ opens the seventh seal. All of heaven is silent. Jesus Christ has left heaven for earth to appear in the clouds to gather his sealed children. The time frame of half an hour equates to one week here on earth. At the sound of the last trump, all the kingdoms of this world become the kingdoms of our Lord (Revelation 11:15). Jesus will return in the clouds as he ascended into the clouds (Acts 1:11). Every person on earth will see the Son of God when the heavens are rolled back (Revelation 1:7). The earth is harvested of the saints who meet Christ in the air. First the dead in Christ rise, then the living in Christ meet them in the air (Revelation 14:15–16, 1 Thessalonians 4:17). The seventh angel pours out its vial of judgment. All the unrepentant who see Christ in the air will be slain. They have blasphemed God and are judged according to their works. They are killed by great hail (Revelation 16:21). No living person will be left to mourn or bury them. They shall be as dung upon the earth (Jeremiah 25:33). The birds will feast upon their dead bodies (Revelation 19:17–18). Then Jesus will declare "it is done" (Revelation 16:17).

Revelation Chapter 20
Eternal Life

Revelation Chapter 20
Eternal Death

What Does This Mean?

> "Blow ye the trumpet in Zion, and sound an alarm in my holy mountain: let all the inhabitants of the land tremble: for the day of the Lord cometh, for it is nigh at hand"
>
> —Joel 2:1

King David and the Apostle Peter declare the Day of the Lord is 1,000 years (Psalm 90:4, 2 Peter 3:8). The Day of the Lord is one of hope and despair. Hope for the righteous because they are resurrected to everlasting life with God in heaven. Despair for the unrighteous because their lack of faith in Christ has doomed them to eternal death. The prophet Joel commands the righteous to be watchmen sounding the alarm to get everyone ready for that day. All decisions are final when the last trumpet sounds.

First Chiasmus

- **Revelation 20:4–6**: "**They lived and reigned with Christ a thousand years. ⁵ But the rest of the dead lived not again until the thousand years were finished.** This the first resurrection. ⁶ **Blessed and holy is he that hath part in the first resurrection**: on such the second death hath no power but they shall be priests of God and of Christ, and shall reign with him a thousand years."

- **Revelation 20:11–13**: "And I saw a great white throne, and him that sat on it, from whose face the earth and the heaven fled away; and there was found no place for them. ¹² And *I saw the dead, small and great, stand before God*; and the books were opened: . . . ¹³ And *the sea gave up the dead which were in it; and death and hell delivered up the dead which were in them: and they were judged every man according to their works.*"

After the Second Coming of Christ, John observes the saints of God living and reigning with Jesus for a thousand years. They are the blessed of God. The unrepentant dead remain in the grave until the thousand years are finished. The unrepentant who were living at the Second Coming of Christ were judged according to their works. They were consumed with the great hail poured out by the seventh angel when the seventh trumpet sounded (Revelation 16:21). Therefore, for the first thousand years after the Second Coming of Christ, no living soul is on earth.

The first resurrection of the saints of God takes place at the Second Coming of Jesus Christ. John sees them sitting on thrones judging and reigning in heaven with Christ for a thousand years. Who or what are they judging?

At this present time man judges other men according to the available evidence. A man is judged a righteous man if his actions and words are righteous. Man's judgment is limited to factual evidence. Man can look and see if the tree bears good or rotten fruit. When the redeemed get to heaven, the saints will look for family members and friends. Not everyone is there who we thought should be, and some will be there, and we will wonder how they got in heaven. Imagine how one will feel if the preacher is not there. Imagine how one will feel if Otis, the town drunk is there. Saints will be confused and filled with great sadness that loved ones are not there. They will wonder why and may question God's judgment.

Earthly man cannot observe or discern the heart or motives of a man. Man does not know nor can he see what God sees when he makes up the jewels for his crown (Zechariah 9:16). Why does God call one a son or daughter, and the other is not? God not only judges the actions or works of man, but He also judges the intent of the heart. God alone knows why people do what they do. God will allow the redeemed to understand His judgment. He will allow the redeemed to understand the "why."

God writes a Book of Remembrance (Malachi 3:16–18), in which He records every action and motive of every man. The book is not for God because He is omniscient. The Book of Remembrance is for those who worship Him and think upon His name. The book is for the redeemed in heaven. God allows His faithful servants to see into His thoughts. God reveals in this book how He knew a person loves, worships, and serves Him.

The thief on the cross next to Jesus will be in heaven. Why? God knew his heart. The man's wicked actions on earth led him to a life of crime. Man judged his actions and sentenced him to death. In a moment of reflection looking in the face of Christ, he saw what he was: a wretched sinner. He repented and believed Jesus was the Son of God. Men saw a criminal. Jesus saw his heart. Jesus forgave him and promised that he would be in paradise with His Lord (Luke 23:39–43).

Earthly men cannot understand the things of God. In heaven, the redeemed will have glorified bodies like Christ's body (Philippians 3:21). The Book of Remembrance is written so that the redeemed can discern what is righteous and wicked. The disciples of Christ who gave up all to follow him for three years saw the thief on the cross. When they see him in heaven, Peter, John, and the others will be allowed to read the Book of Remembrance. They, too, will see the heart of the thief that God saw and will understand why he is in heaven as they are. They will know that God's judgment is true.

All the redeemed will search the books for answers to learn more about God. The heart of every man will be revealed. Everyone in His presence is there because each one had responded from his heart to God's love and guidance. Saints will be totally assured that all God's judgments are true.

"But the rest of the dead lived not again until the thousand years were finished." After the thousand years are finished, the graves and the sea will give up the dead that are in them. This is the resurrection of the unrepentant. John sees the dead stand before the great white throne of God, and the books are opened. God reads the Book of Remembrance to judge every man according to their works. The Book of Life is opened. The names of the dead are not found in the Book of Life, so "there was found no place for them" in heaven. God's judgments are true.

Second Chiasmus

- **Revelation 20:2:** "And **he laid hold on the dragon, that old serpent, which is the Devil, and Satan, and bound him a thousand years.**"

- **Revelation 20:7:** "And *when the thousand years are expired, Satan shall be loosed out of his prison.*"

The lost dead remain in the grave for a thousand years. John now describes what will happen to Satan during the thousand years.

First, John sees an angel come down from heaven with a great chain and the key to the bottomless pit. In Revelation Chapter 9, Satan was given the key to the bottomless pit to deceive the nations. This angel from Chapter 20 comes to close the pit of deception. The angel lays hold on Satan, and he is bound a thousand years. No longer can he deceive the nations because there are no nations to deceive. Everyone who had rejected the Savior was destroyed at the brightness of His Second Coming. Satan will roam an uninhabited, desolate earth for one thousand years.

After the thousand years are completed, Satan must be loosed for a little time when the unrepentant dead are resurrected. Satan will gather his army of the unrepentant, resurrected ones to battle God one last time. This is the battle of Gog and Magog. The Great Deceiver will deceive the nations one last time into thinking they can overtake the City of God, New Jerusalem.

Third Chiasmus

- **Revelation 20:9: "And they went up on the breadth of the earth, and compassed the camp of the saints about, and the beloved city: and fire came down from God out of heaven, and devoured them."**

- **Revelation 20:14–15**: *"And death and hell were cast into the lake of fire. This is the second death. ¹⁵ And whosoever was not found written in the book of life was cast into the lake of fire."*

John describes the multitude rising from the dead as the sand of the sea. These were those in the graves who did not see Jesus at the Second Coming. Millions of unrepentant souls rise from their slumber in the same corrupted state as they entered the grave. Their works continue to manifest their unworthiness for eternal life in heaven. Satan and the risen dead see the holy city of God, New Jerusalem, descending from heaven. Satan rallies his troops of unbelievers for one final battle to overtake the saints of God and the beloved city, New Jerusalem.

Satan deceives them into believing that the One sitting on the Great White Throne is the reason they cannot access the city. That is the great lie. God had done all He could for all men to inherit eternal life. They had rejected God's grace while they were living, and now the consequence of that rejection enrages them. The inhabitants of New Jerusalem are watching the battle unfold. They get their first look at Satan and ask, "Is this the man that made the earth to tremble, that did shake kingdoms?" (Isaiah 14:16). The redeemed cannot understand how this creature caused so much destruction.

The unquenchable fire falling down from God out of heaven instantly devours them. Immediately, the heavens and the earth explode and are burned up (2 Peter 3:10). All the wicked shall be as logs for the bonfire. Satan and all the enemies of God will be consumed leaving nothing but ashes to be walked upon (Malachi 4:1–3). They shall be as if they had never been (Obadiah 15–16). This is the second death.

Revelation Chapters 2 and 3
Promises Made

Revelation Chapters 21 and 22
Promises Fulfilled

What Does This Mean?

The Great Commission, Matthew 28:18–20, applies to all true churches of Christ for all time. Jesus instructs His churches to go into all the world and teach the gospel to everyone, make disciples or believers, baptize them, and instruct them to continue the process of establishing churches and making new converts.

The seven Churches of Revelation Chapters 2 and 3 represent the 2,000-plus-year history of churches from John, the writer of Revelation, until Jesus Christ returns. These were literal churches located in the cities mentioned, and each letter describes an historical period. The assigned dates may not be exact, but are an approximate date of the described historical event and the dates are generally accepted by church historians. Jesus gives to the churches a commendation, a condemnation, and a promise. Each church had a set of challenges that are relevant for all churches at all times. All churches should heed the commendations, condemnations, and promises made by Jesus.

The Chiasmus verses in these chapters will either complement or contrast each other. A brief history is given for each church period.

The Church of Ephesus: Revelation 2:1–7

The book of Acts records the history of the first churches. The Church at Ephesus represents the Apostolic Church Period from AD 33–100. After the ascension of Jesus Christ, the empowering of the Holy Spirit came upon the first church in Jerusalem. Peter preached his first sermon explaining the events of Jesus Christ's crucifixion and resurrection, which the people of Jerusalem had witnessed. Three thousand souls were added to the first church in Jerusalem. Many more who trusted Jesus Christ as their Savior were added daily. On another occasion, over five thousand were added to the church in Jerusalem.

The church of the first century had great zeal and love for the Lord in spite of persecutions from unbelieving Jews in Jerusalem. Converts from Jerusalem carried the gospel to families and friends in other towns. Churches began to grow as the church in Jerusalem had grown. Because of this very rapid growth, many paganistic beliefs began to enter the congregations of the churches. Jesus commended them for staying true to the doctrines of the Word of God. This first church hated the deeds of the Nicolaitans, which is the rule or authority of the pastor or priest. Jesus gave them a warning to continue loving Him and to keep His commandments and teachings. This warning continues to apply to all His churches.

First Chiasmus

- **Revelation 2:7**: "He that hath an ear, let him hear what the Spirit saith unto the churches: **To him that overcometh, will I give to eat of the tree of life**, which is in the midst of the paradise of God."

- **Revelation 22:14**: "Blessed are *they that do his commandments*, that *they may have right to the tree of life*, and may enter in through the gates into the city."

- **Revelation 21:7**: "*He that overcometh shall inherit all things.*"

The Apostolic Church Period experienced great growing pains. Jews and Gentiles were believing the gospel of Christ. However, both wanted to continue in the works of faith they had always known. The Jewish believers wanted to continue the ceremonial feasts and ceremonial laws of Moses. The

Gentile believers wanted to add their superstitions of spiritism and Gnosticism to the church worship service. Some who were joining the church did not believe that Jesus Christ was the Son of the God, the Savior of man. These conflicting beliefs caused much confusion. Jesus instructs this church age and all churches to "Remember therefore from whence thou art fallen, and repent, and do the first works" (Revelation 2:5).

Jesus promises the overcomer eternal life (Revelation 2:7) for their faith and obedience to the commandments. Who are the overcomers?

The overcomers believe that Jesus is the Son of God (1 John 5:5). They confess that their sins are paid by the blood of the Lamb. They hold fast to their confession and will not change their mind (Revelation 12:11). The overcomers continue to keep the commandments of God and the faith of Jesus all their life. Their character reflects Christ (Revelation 14:12). God gave his Ten Commandments to man to perform (Deuteronomy 4:13). Jesus told his disciples that keeping the commandments was as act of love to God (John 14:15).

According to Jesus, an overcomer is one who recognizes Jesus Christ not only as his Savior, but as his Lord.

The Church in Smyrna: Revelation 2:8–11

The Church in Smyrna represents the Persecuted Church Period from 100–313. The Roman Emperors became worried about the popularity of Christianity because they considered themselves gods. Laws or edicts were passed allowing the persecution of Christian heretics. Roman Emperor Nero fed many Christians to the lions as sport in the Roman Colosseum. Roman Emperor Diocletian led one of the most severe persecutions of Christians beginning in 303 and ending in 313. Jesus revealed this time of fierce persecution to John in Revelation 2:10. In spite of the tribulation, the church remained faithful, and the gospel continued to spread across the Roman Empire. Jesus recognized their faithfulness and promised them a crown of life. Even though many had been killed by wicked men, the faithful saints would not experience the second death.

Second Chiasmus

- **Revelation 2:10–11**: "Ye **shall have tribulation ten days** . . . [11] He that hath an ear, let him hear what the Spirit saith unto the churches; **He that overcometh shall not be hurt of the second death**."

- **Revelation 21:7, 8**: "He that overcometh shall inherit all things; and I will be his God, and he shall be my son. *But the fearful, and unbelieving, and the abominable, and murderers, and whoremongers, and sorcerers, and idolaters, and all liars, shall have their part in the lake which burneth with fire and brimstone: which is the second death*."

Roman Emperor Diocletian and many other men of authority did all they could to eliminate Christianity. The lion's den, torture, and burning Christians at the stake became common place. Many scrolls and parchments containing the Scriptures were destroyed. Smyrna represents the beginning of this time of trouble. Persecution of God's people continued for centuries. In spite of Satan's efforts to eliminate Christianity, the gospel spread throughout the world because of the overcomers' faith and obedience to Jesus Christ.

Jesus knew this terrible persecution was coming. Jesus told John to write that although they may face death for their belief, they shall not be hurt of the second death (Revelation 20:6). But the fearful, unbelieving, abominable sinners shall have their part in the lake which burns with fire and brimstone which is the second death. They shall be as they never were (Obadiah 15, 16).

The Church in Pergamos: Revelation 2:12–17

The Church at Pergamos represents the State Church Period from 313–538. Constantine became the Emperor of Rome in 313. He declared religious tolerance, which was a time of false peace for Christians. Emperor Constantine also declared that he was Pontifex Maximus, the head of the church and its chief high priest, thereby taking the place of Jesus Christ. Satan takes "a seat" and "dwelleth" in Constantine's state-sponsored church (Revelation 2:13). Satan gave Emperor Constantine his power and authority (Revelation 13:2).

Emperor Constantine declared many edicts and church councils giving the Roman Church the authority to declare worship, doctrine, and dogma. The Roman Empire enforced the apostate church's doctrine, rooted out heresy, and upheld ecclesiastical unity. A marriage of church and state occurred, usurping Christ's authority over His Church. This unholy union of church and state instituted the doctrines of Balaam and the Nicolaitans.

Balaam was a false prophet of God (Numbers 24–31). Balaam counseled the sons of the Moabites, the enemies of God, to marry the daughters of Israel, the people of God. Through this union of believer and unbeliever, paganism was introduced to the people of God. The people of God began to worship idols rather than God. The doctrine of Balaam is mixing truth with error. If the smallest error is introduced to truth, then truth is no longer truth, but a mixing or "fornication" of truth.

The doctrine of the Nicolaitans is pastor rule or authority over the church. During this time in church history, the priest assumed the role of the head of the church. The priest in the church at Rome declared himself the vicar or representative of Christ on earth. The church taught that the priest was the only one who could understand and interpret the Word of God for the congregation; his words were God's words. The doctrine of the Nicolaitans evolved into the heretical teachings of infallibility of the pope, absolution of sins by the priest, and authority of the doctrines and traditions of the church over the Word of God.

In the early history of the church, the manuscripts of the holy Scriptures were rare. The priest was the authority because he had the Scriptures. Today, Bibles are widely available, and every person can search the Scriptures. The Holy Spirit of God guides everyone to truth. No man will stand before God and blame another for his sins. The subversion of authority of Christ by the priest cannot be claimed as a reason for unbelief when being judged by Christ. A member of the church cannot say, "the pastor said, or the church forgave" as a reason for not having the faith of Christ and keeping the commandments of God (Revelation 14:12). Jesus commended the first church in Ephesus for hating the deeds of the Nicolaitans and He emphatically stated, "which I also hate" (Revelation 2:14–15).

Jesus Christ is the head of the church, not the pastor, priest, or pope (Colossians 1:18). These two doctrines of Balaam and the Nicolaitans replaced the atoning sacrifice of Jesus Christ with idols, works of man, and church/pastor authority. The true believers of Christ in the true church of Christ rejected these doctrines and were pushed further into isolation, hiding in caves and in the mountains. Therefore, during this historical period, the church split into two groups: those who believed the Word of God and those who believed the teachings and tradition of man. True believers were given many names: Montanists, Donatists, Novatians, and Waldenses. The false church later became known as the Roman Catholic Church with the pope as the head, its chief high priest and the keeper of their faith.

Third Chiasmus

- **Revelation 2:17**: "He that hath an ear, let him hear what the Spirit saith unto the churches; **To him that overcometh** will I give to eat of the hidden manna, and **will give him a white stone**, and **in the stone a new name written**, which no man knoweth saving he that receiveth it."

- **Revelation 21:9–10**: "And there came unto me one of the seven angels which had the seven vials full of the seven last plagues, and talked with me, saying, Come hither, I will shew thee *the bride, the Lamb's wife.* [10] And he carried me away in the spirit to a great and high mountain, and *shewed me that great city, the holy Jerusalem*, descending out of heaven from God.

- **Revelation 22:4**: "And they shall see his face; and *his name shall be in their foreheads.*"

- **Revelation 21:7**: "*He that overcometh shall inherit all things.*"

The Pergamos historical period was a very dangerous time for the Lord's churches. The false doctrine replacing Jesus Christ as the chief high priest and head of the church could have destroyed the early church forever. Satan covets worship, and he had found a place in this political/religious organization in Rome under the leadership of Emperor Constantine where he could control worship.

White stones were used to build Solomon's Temple in Jerusalem. The stones were fit together to make a glorious, beautiful temple worthy of Jesus Christ. Church members are referred to as stones fitted together to glorify Jesus Christ (1 Peter 2:5).

God uses ordinary people to build His kingdom of believers. The ordinary people of this historical period accomplished an extraordinary work. They believed God's Word and protected the gospel of Christ despite a maze of heretical doctrines. For their efforts, they were banished from society and severely persecuted even, in some cases, put to death. Jesus Christ commends them and promises they will be stones in His kingdom. Their names are lost to history, but Jesus Christ knows every one of them by name.

One day these overcomers and all believers who hold fast to the faith of Jesus Christ will be part of the bride, the Lamb's wife, joined with the blessed Savior forever in New Jerusalem in God's heavenly kingdom. The overcomers in Christ who have his name in their minds and hearts will enjoy these blessings forever.

The Church in Thyatira: Revelation 2:18–29:

The Church in Thyatira represents the Papal Church Period from 538 to 1517. This period is the longest church period and covers most of the "great tribulation" or Dark Ages, as it is known in history. The prophet Daniel foretold of this time and said that it would last for 1,260 years (Daniel 7:25).

During this period, the Pope of the Roman Catholic

Church was declared the Pontifex Maximus. The Justinian Code was enacted at this time. (See notes from Revelation 13:1–2.) The Pope in Rome, acting as head of the church and its chief high priest, also assumed secular authority over state governments. The false church not only assumed power to change God's laws and His Word, but also assumed the political power to enforce the changed laws. Anyone not following the Roman Catholic Church was labeled a heretic, which was punishable by death. God's true believers were hunted, persecuted, and killed by the millions.

Jesus compares this false church to "that woman Jezebel, which calleth herself a prophetess, to teach and to seduce my servants to commit fornication, and to eat things sacrificed unto idols" (Revelation 2:20). Babylonian paganism engulfed this false system of worship. Also, during this period, the Ottoman Empire warred with the church of Rome. Many fled into Europe with the philosophy of Plato, Socrates, and Aristotle, bringing the "Age of Reason" to Europe. God's salvation, His Word, and His Spirit were withheld from the people. This was a very dark, dangerous time for the true church of Jesus Christ.

Jesus reassured His people that His Word would revive. John Wycliffe, the "Morning Star" of the Reformation (Revelation 2:28), was instrumental in getting the Bible translated into the language of the common people. Light was beginning to enter the darkness. The Word of God empowered by the Spirit of God continued to testify of God's love and power. Men continued to trust God for salvation and deliverance. Churches continued to expand across the continents spreading the gospel of Christ.

Fourth Chiasmus

- **Revelation 2:26–27: "And he that overcometh, and keepeth my works unto the end, to him will I give power over the nations: [27] And he shall rule them with a rod of iron.**

- **Revelation 19:15: "*He shall rule them with a rod of iron*."**

- **Revelation 22:5: "*And they shall reign for ever and ever.*"**

- **Revelation 21:7: "*He that overcometh shall inherit all things.*"**

The Word of God is compared to a rod of iron. God rules with an iron rod. Man rules with an iron fist. Iron does not bend. Neither will God's Word bend nor can it be changed by man. Truth is always straight as a rod. Believers who have the faith of Jesus Christ and keep his commandments will not bend to error and worship the mark or the teachings of the false religious beast system. Throughout the Dark Ages, God's people kept the faith. The truth of God's Word emerged from this awful period just as pure as it had entered.

Jesus Christ promises overcomers that He will give them power to rule over the nations. They will pass judgment on the false religious system that beheaded them for their witness of Jesus Christ. The overcomers in Christ will inherit all things in heaven where they shall reign forever with their Lord and Savior, Jesus Christ.

The Church in Sardis: Revelation 3:1-7

The Church in Sardis represents the Reformed Church Period from 1517 to 1755. The Reformation of the false church begins during this period. Careful reading of the Scriptures convinced Catholic priests such as Luther, Calvin, Wycliffe, Wesley, and others that Jesus alone, Faith alone, and the Word alone is the Way to God. The early reformers identified the Pope of the Roman Catholic Church as the Antichrist and began to push back against the false doctrines of the Roman Church such as salvation by works, penance, and indulgences. Martin Luther taught that salvation is by grace, not works. John Calvin was convinced from the Scriptures that men had freedom of conscience to believe and trust God without dictates from the church or state. John Wesley preached the Lordship of Jesus Christ in believers' lives. The Reformers found Christ to be the authority of the Bible, not the church or priests. These brave men also translated the Bible from Latin into the common languages of the people. In 1611, the King James or Authorized Version of the Old and New Testaments was printed as the Bible for English-speaking people.

Satan was not at rest during this time of awakening of the Scriptures. During this period, the Jesuits used the

Inquisitions to persecute the reformers and "heretics" in some of the most gruesome methods ever recorded in history. Many believers in Christ left Europe for America seeking religious freedom. The Dark Ages of the Great Tribulation period for the true church of Christ was ending but not without a high cost.

Fifth Chiasmus

- **Revelation 3:4–5**: "Thou has a few names even in Sardis and **they shall walk with me in white: for they are worthy.** ⁵ **He that overcometh**, the same **shall be clothed in white raiment; and I will not blot out his name out of the book of life.**"

- **Revelation 19:8**: "And to her was granted that *she should be arrayed in fine line, clean and white: for the fine linen is the righteousness of saints.*"

- **Revelation 21:27**: "And there shall in no wise enter into it any thing that defileth: but *they which are written in the Lamb's book of life.*"

- **Revelation 21:7**: "*He that overcometh shall inherit all things.*"

The biblical doctrine of salvation by grace through faith became very precious to the early reformers (Ephesians

2:8–9). These brave men read the Bible and believed that salvation came from the sacrifice of Jesus Christ on the cross of Calvary and not from penance or the treasury of merit. God's grace and love for man brought Jesus to earth to pay the sin debt that man could not pay. No payment of indulgences or penance could ever pay the price of sin. The only righteousness that man can have is the righteousness of Jesus Christ.

Salvation in Jesus Christ cost these saints of God dearly. The Reformers were martyred for protesting against the established church. The common people took notice and took up the banner of the cross following Jesus Christ as their Savior. Many believed the gospel of Christ and left the false church. For their faith, God counted them worthy, and their names are recorded in the Lamb's Book of Life. Only those written in the Lamb's Book of Life are clothed in white linen; the righteous of the saints, are allowed into the presence of God to inherit all things.

Believers, thank God for the testimony and faith of our forefathers. Our prayer is that in our day of trouble, we will be counted worthy.

The Church in Philadelphia: Revelation 3:7–13

The Church in Philadelphia represents the Missionary Church Period from 1755 to 1888. The 1,260 years of tribulation had ended, and the famine of the gospel was over. Many Bible colleges and societies emerged in many countries. Men of God were focused on printing, studying, commenting, and preaching the Word of God. Churches were sending missionaries worldwide to proclaim the gospel, and new churches were planted worldwide. The Church experienced a true time of revival. This age also saw the writing of the US Bill of Rights to secure the observance of religious freedom and freedom of conscience.

This historical period was also perilous for the newfound freedom of the church. Civil War in the United States threatened the newly established freedoms, and the French Revolution denounced all religion for the citizens. Reason and philosophy became the gods of man. The beginnings of Communism and Darwin's theory of evolution questioned the Bible's account of creation, sowing seeds of doubt about the heavenly Creator. The discovery of lost, spurious manuscripts of the Scriptures questioned the validity of God's Word. Textual critics Westcott and Hort declared the latter manuscripts of the Syriac Sinaiticus and Codex Vaticanus superior to the authorized text of the King James Bible.

Also, during this time, the Second Coming of Jesus Christ began to be studied and preached. Sincere men of faith made predictions about the exact day of the Second Coming. These predictions proved to be false causing believers and unbelievers to mock and doubt the creation, God's Word, and the truth of His Second Coming. God's faithful followers had to cling more than ever to God and His Word.

Sixth Chiasmus

- **Revelation 3:11–12**: "**Behold, I come quickly**: hold that fast which thou hast, **that no man take thy crown.** [12] **Him that overcometh** will I make a pillar **in the temple of my God**, and **I will write upon him the name of my God**, and the name of the city of my God, which is **new Jerusalem, and I will write upon him my new name.**"

- **Revelation 22:20**: "*Surely I come quickly.*"

- **Revelation 22:5**: "*And they shall reign for ever and ever.*"

- **Revelation 21:22**: "For the *Lord God Almighty and the Lamb are the temple of it.*"

- **Revelation 21:10**: "That great city, *the holy Jerusalem*, descending out of heaven."

- **Revelation 22:4**: "And they shall see his face; and *his name shall be in their foreheads.*"

- **Revelation 21:7**: "*He that overcometh shall inherit all things.*"

Jesus Christ assures the overcomers that His promises are true. He is coming quickly, hold tightly to the faith, and do not deny His power, His Word, or His promises. Jesus promises them a new name; a new city, Jerusalem; a crown;

and a throne. Believers look forward to the return of their Savior and Hope, Jesus Christ.

The Church of the Laodiceans: Revelation 3:14–22

The Church of the Laodiceans represents the Apostate Church Period from 1888 to the Second Coming of Jesus Christ. The last church letter penned by John represents the condition of the present-day church. At the close of this church period, Jesus Christ comes again, and time is no more on this earth. God's people have been set free from persecution and have taken advantage of their liberty in Christ.

The salutation of this letter (verse 14) is very telling. Jesus is reminding His people that He is the Amen, the final authority of good and evil and right and wrong. He is also the faithful and true witness. Jesus has never abandoned those who love and obey Him. His words are always truth whether man wants to hear and believe them or not. Jesus also reminds the members of this last church period that He is the Creator. He was in the beginning with God. He is God (John 1:1–5).

During this period, God's Word has been polluted with spurious manuscripts that tempt God's people to question the true Word of God. Many versions of the Bible began to be printed all claiming to be the "truth." Different versions of the Bible justify every belief of man. Man is now God's equal. According to their thinking, "God is Love," which means He must not only tolerate but accept every action or work of man. The Word of God is no longer the authority for good or evil; man's philosophy is the guide. Jesus tells this last-day church that their works are neither cold or hot (verses 15–16). Man has an indifference to God's Word. Jesus says, "I will spue thee out of my mouth." He is not pleased with man's indifference.

Church members see themselves as "rich, and increased with goods, and having need of nothing." But God sees them as "wretched, and miserable, and poor, and blind, and naked" (verse 17). Pursuits of wealth and happiness occupy so much time leaving people empty and broken. Jesus told a parable of a rich young man who came to Him asking what he could do to have eternal life (Matthew 19:16–22). Jesus instructed him to obey the law of God. The rich young man told Jesus that he already obeyed the law, so what did he lack? Jesus told him to sell all he had, give to the poor, and "come and follow me." The man went away sorrowful. He was not willing to trust Christ over his riches; he loved his life more than God.

That parable describes the Church of Laodicea, which is the high self-esteem church. Members love this world and all its charms more than they love God. Jesus counsels this church to buy of Him gold, white raiment, and eye salve (verse 18). Where can man buy those items? That is the point. Man cannot buy his way into heaven into the presence of God (Isaiah 55:1–3). Jesus Christ paid the price. God desires for all to believe in Him, trust Him, and receive from Him everlasting life.

New forms of worship have been introduced into today's

church. New cultural values are embraced, and the commandments of God are ignored. Jesus is outside His church knocking on the door pleading to enter into the midst of His people. Jesus Christ loves the Church of Laodicea and has not given up on her.

Seventh Chiasmus

- **Revelation 3:18, 21**: "And **white raiment**, ... [21] **To him that overcometh** will I grant to **sit with me in my throne**."

- **Revelation 19:8**: "*Fine linen, clean and white*."

- **Revelation 20:4**: "And *I saw thrones*."

- **Revelation 21:7**: "*He that overcometh shall inherit all things*."

The overcomers in the Church of Laodicea are those who open the door of their hearts and accept Jesus Christ's plea to enter. They will be arrayed in the white raiment of Christ's righteousness. The time to open the door of your heart to Christ is now. Today is the day of salvation. Choose Christ and his righteousness.

God gives every man freedom of conscience and freedom of choice. God will not force anyone to believe Him, accept His free pardon of sin, and obey Him. Unbelievers make a choice to embrace a false system of religion empowered by Satan; they reject God's great love and mercy for man. The scoffers and unbelievers reject God's plan of salvation. They reject God's grace through faith in Jesus Christ (Ephesians 2:8–9). They reject Jesus Christ as their sacrifice for sin. They reject the truth of God's Holy Word. Therefore, they reject eternal life and will be cast into the lake of fire, which is the second death (Revelation 20:14).

Revelation Chapter 1
The First and the Last

Revelation Chapter 22
The Beginning and the End

What Does This Mean?

We end our study with the beginning and the end, the first and the last, the alpha and the omega, Jesus Christ. If you have read up to this point, we thank you. In this last chapter, we want to talk to you from our hearts.

First Chiasmus

- **Revelation 1:3: "Blessed is he that readeth, and they that hear the words of this prophecy."**

- **Revelation 22:7**: "*Blessed is he that keepeth the sayings of the prophecy of this book.*"

Jesus tells John that reading, hearing, and believing the words of this prophecy are a blessing. As the authors of this little book, we can only say Amen. Reading, studying, and writing this little book has been a blessing. We want to tell you about our journey.

The book of Revelation is the one book of the Bible that people seem to be interested in knowing what it says. "Tell me what it says" is the response of most Christians. But few people desire to study it; most think the book cannot be understood.

We were those people. We had always read the book as most people do from Chapter 1 to Chapter 22 using the cross-reference Scriptures from the Bible. We would have almost as many questions at the end of the study as we had at the beginning. In the fall of 2023, Russell was scrolling the internet when he saw a chart outlining the chapters of Revelation using the chiastic structure. We had never heard of chiastic structure.

We began a family Bible study on the book of Revelation putting ideas together as a chiasmus. We noticed that many phrases and descriptions of Christ in Revelation 1 and 22 repeat. The more we studied, the more we began to see the chiasmus verses. We were not reading chapters and verses, but topics, descriptions, time periods describing the same events. We were following the prophet Isaiah studying precept by precept and line by line. The more we cross-referenced Scriptures, the clearer the meaning of the Scriptures became.

In the summer of 2024, I (Shirley) taught a series of lessons about the History of the Church. I researched many historical events and people. In sharing my lessons with Russell, we discovered that the historical events of the church fit perfectly with the prophesied events in the book of Revelation. The Scriptures were becoming clearer. Jesus was absolutely right: We were blessed! We wanted to share the message with others. So, we did, and no one knew what we were talking about. Chiastic structure! What?

Now, here we are two years later writing this book. We do not dare think we have all knowledge and understanding of the book of Revelation. We simply want to bring the same joy to our readers that we have received from reading and studying the Revelation using the chiastic structure, reference Scriptures, and historical events. It is comforting to know where we are in the timeline of history.

The next events will occur very rapidly. How are we to be the watchman on the tower if we have not read the book of Revelation? Christ is depending on the faithful to sound the alarm in these last days. Jesus Christ is coming soon! All need to repent, believe in God's love and mercy and grace. Believe Jesus Christ died for your sins. Trust Him as your Savior. Live a life of obedience to Him.

Why do churches today shy away from teaching the book of Revelation? Many believe there will be a kingdom set up here on earth by Christ or his representatives and that all things will be understood then. If that was the case, then when Christ came forth out of the tomb, He had every right to establish an earthly kingdom. The grave was defeated, and sin was conquered. Christ was the King. Even the apostles were still asking about the kingdom at His ascension.

But Christ said His kingdom is not of this world. His kingdom is a heavenly kingdom. He has gone to prepare a place for us, and He will come again and take us to that place prepared for those who love Him. Since His kingdom is not of this world, this world will never be utopia. No one should be looking for an earthly kingdom, but for the heavenly kingdom promised by Christ.

Another reason churches don't study this book of Revelation is that many believe the church will be gone during the bad stuff. If the church is in heaven during the tribulation, then why study the book? They think, "It is of no use and no one can understand it anyway." The faithful church members of Smyrna, Pergamos, Thyatira, and Sardis would need to speak to the manager about this claim. These Church ages went through the height of the Great Tribulation and were slaughtered by the millions. According to the belief that the faithful escape the tribulation, those churches should have been removed from the wrath for their faithfulness.

Psalm 91 speaks of the faithful saints watching the destruction happen in front of their eyes. The saints declare that God is their refuge and strength. We should not fear what man does to us because His eyes are on the wicked.

He gives His angels charge over His children. He will set His loved ones on high because He knows their names. We believe God by faith. The book of Revelation is a blessing and should be read, taught, and believed by all Christians.

Second Chiasmus

- **Revelation 1:7: "Behold, he cometh with clouds; and every eye shall see him . . . all kindreds of the earth shall wail because of him. Even so, Amen."**

- **Revelation 22:12**: "And, *behold, I come quickly*; and *my reward is with me, to give every man according as his work shall be.*"

Jesus Christ assures John and the churches that He is coming in the clouds just as He ascended into heaven (Acts 1:11b).

Every eye shall see Him when Christ appears with the clouds. No one will miss His appearing. Those who "pierced him" or rejected His claim as Messiah, the Savior of mankind, will wail or be very alarmed, fearful and angry at His coming. They refused Jesus Christ's work on the cross paying the sin debt. Unbelievers will be judged and rewarded according to their works because they refused the invitation to "Come" and drink the water of life freely. They refused to obey God and will try to hide at His coming (Revelation 6:16–17). Those who blasphemed God will be killed by the great hail falling from heaven (Revelation 16:21). They will be consumed by the brightness of His coming (2 Thessalonians 2:8). They shall be as if they had never been (Obadiah 15–16).

Jesus assures John and the churches that He is coming quickly and is bringing His reward with Him. The believer's reward is eternal life with God. The saints who are in the grave will rise to life eternal, and the living saints at His appearing will meet them in the clouds (2 Thessalonians 4:16–17).

Our Final Thoughts . . . What Happens Next?

We believe the last prophetic events, the worship of the image of the beast and the mark of the beast of Revelation 13, are on the horizon. All other prophecies have been fulfilled. We believe, as the Reformers believed, that the Roman Catholic Church is the first beast of Revelation 13. We have established that the second beast is the United States of America. In the future, these two beast systems will merge. We believe the Roman Catholic Church along with the United States of America will fulfill the prophecy of Revelation 13 by supplying the remedy for the world's problems. We have shown through the words of the leaders of the Roman Catholic Church that her "mark" of authority is the establishment of Sunday as the day of worship. We believe this "mark of the beast" will be used as the solution for the world's problems.

The United States is already giving preeminence to Sunday as the day of worship. Mandate for Leadership Project 2025 on page 589 encourages Congress to amend the Fair

Labor Standards Act to mandate overtime pay on Sunday. The passage of that law will cause an undue burden to all businesses open on Sunday. In the case of Groff v. Dejoy, the Supreme Court ruled in June 2023 that employees desiring to worship on Sunday must be accommodated. Many around the world are advocating for a day of rest for the earth and family.

Our world is a place of unrest. In the future, events will occur that will cause the citizens of the world to look for relief. The events may be war, famine, disease, weather disasters, or combinations of many catastrophes that cause people to look to leaders of faith or in government for the solutions. We believe the Roman Catholic Church will unite with the United States government to provide the rest and relief the citizens of the world desperately desire. A day of rest will become the law of the world for the common good of all men. All businesses will be forced to close on Sunday. All citizens, believers or unbelievers, will be forced to worship on Sunday. When the mark of the beast, Sunday worship, becomes the law of the land, and all men are forced to worship the image of the beast, the time of trouble begins.

All citizens of the world, famous or unknown, rich or poor, business owner or laborer will be required to rest and worship on the first day of the week, Sunday. All who refuse and do not submit to the authority of the world-wide government sponsored day of rest and worship will not be allowed to buy or sell. Before COVID-19, the idea that a person could not buy or sell was preposterous. Now the citizens of the world understand very well how the government can close businesses, freeze bank accounts, cancel school, and totally remove freedom of movement and conscience. The law will affect everyone and all will be required to obey. Every facet of life will be controlled by the governments: employment, education, food, energy, worship. For those who choose to disobey, a slow death of starvation may occur.

The seven last plagues will begin when the mark is made the law of the land. We believe those plagues will be poured out over the span of one year. At the end of that year, the Roman Catholic Church, as well as all religion and the Bible, will be abolished as it was in the French Revolution. This is a strange statement to make. The government mandates a church sponsored day of worship, then abolishes the church and all religion. The government leaders now see themselves as Constantine and Justinian saw themselves: *Pontifex Maximus*. The state is now the Head of the Church and its High Priest. The governments of the world are totally controlled by Satan. The world is his kingdom and no mention of God is allowed. Men are now gods with every imagination of their heart continually evil.

We have several reasons for believing the end is near. The last empire in the Bible is the United States of America. As much as we love this country, it is fading as all worldly empires do. Internal strife, lawlessness, economic decline, and tremendous debt plagues our country. The glory years are past; the nation is in the survival stage. The church of Laodicea is the last church age. This age began in the 1800s and will continue until Christ returns. The church of Laodicea is growing weaker; it is becoming more of a remnant than a conquering church. The most startling sign that we observe is the low birth rate around the globe; we believe God is protecting the innocent before the time of plagues begins. The "great falling away" spoken of by the Apostle Paul has happened. Men and women do not understand their role in protecting a home, church, society, or civilization. God's arms are open wide pleading to all to turn to Him.

> "As I live, saith the Lord God, I have no pleasure in the death of the wicked; but that the wicked turn from his way and live: turn ye, turn ye from your evil way; for why will ye die?"
>
> —Ezekiel 33:11

Shortly after these events, Jesus Christ will appear in the clouds to take the remnant believers to heaven. The length of time between the destruction of the whore of Babylon and the return of Christ is unknown. But we do have a promise that He will shorten the days for the elect. We also have the promise that God will provide for and protect the remnant of faithful believers at this time. They will not escape this terrible time of trouble, but God will see them through. Just as the faithful Christians lived through the horrible Dark Ages and would not compromise faith in Christ, the faithful remnant will not take the mark of the beast or worship his image. They will continue to obey the commandments of God and keep the faith of their Lord and Savior Jesus Christ. They will love God and believe His promises more than their lives on this sin wrecked planet.

We have inherited lies. Satan is a great deceiver and has deceived many throughout the years. We believe in the 1800's, knowledge was hidden. Every generation since believed and taught what they had been taught. We love and respect every preacher and teacher we have known. Our purpose is not confusion or division. Through much prayer, careful study of the Word and history, we have come to these conclusions. God's Word must be believed. Jesus Christ is the Way to heaven. God's commandments must be kept. Jesus says, "If you love me, keep my commandments" (John 14:15). This is the time for all to make the decision to believe and stand for God.

> "Surely I come quickly. Amen. Even so, come Lord Jesus. The grace of our Lord Jesus Christ be with you all. Amen."
>
> —Revelation 22:20–21

Notes

1 Keum Young Ahn, Gerard Damsteegt, Edwin de Kock, et al., "538 A.D. and the Transition from Pagan Roman Empire to Holy Roman Empire: Justinian's Metamorphosis from Chief of Staffs to Theologian," International Journal of Humanities and Social Science 7, no. 1 (2017), https://www.ijhssnet.com/journals/Vol_7_No_1_January_2017/7.pdf.

2 The Catholic Record, September 1, 1923.

3 Cardinal Gibbon, The Catholic Mirror, December 23, 1893.

4 Priest Brady, in an address at Elizabeth, New Jersey, on March 17, 1903, (in Elizabeth News, March 18, 1903).

5 Philip Schaff, History of the Christian Church: Vol. II: From Constantine the Great to Gregory the Great A.D. 311–600(New York: Charles Scribner, 1867), 380n1.

6 The History of the Decline and Fall of the Roman empire, III, 370

7 Martin Luther, On War Against the Turk (1529), in "The Turk is the rod of the wrath of the Lord our God and the servant of the raging Devil," quoted in Trevor Castor, Martin

Luther on Islam and "the Turks", Zwemer Center for Muslim Studies (n.d.), accessed August 21, 2025.

8 "Lisbon Earthquake of 1755." Encyclopaedia Britannica. Accessed August 21, 2025. https://www.britannica.com/event/Lisbon-earthquake-of-1755

9 Samuel Williams, "An Account of a Very Uncommon Darkness in the States of NewEngland, May 19, 1780," Memoirs of the American Academy of Arts and Sciences 1 (1783): 234–36.

10 How Newspapers Helped Crowdsource a Scientific Discovery: The 1833 Leonid Meteor Storm. September 2, 2020. Posted by: Malea Walker. blogs.loc.gov

About the Authors

Connect with us at chiasticbook@gmail.com

Russell McCann is a stay-at-home dad who has dedicated the past several years to studying the Word of God, seeking to make complex truths accessible through a clear, common-sense approach. Each day, he turns to Scripture for guidance and insight, weaving what he learns into a message of faith and understanding that he now shares in this book.

A lifelong resident of North Louisiana, Russell has been married for more than 20 years and is the proud father of three children. When he isn't reading, writing, or reflecting on Scripture, he can often be found piddling in the garden—or simply trying to stay cool in the Louisiana heat.

Shirley McCann has been married to her husband for 48 years and is the proud mother of two and "Sugar" to six grandchildren. A retired elementary school teacher with 25 years in the classroom, she now devotes her time to her church, where she teaches a ladies' class and plays the piano.

Shirley loves to read, travel with family and friends, and spend quiet moments at the cabin on the lake—her favorite place to relax and reflect.